Cricketers of My Time

The Daily Telegraph

Cricketers of My Time

Heroes to Remember

E. W. Swanton

André Deutsch

For my friend Hugh Massingberd
Author, editor and obituarist

First published in Great Britain in 1999 by
André Deutsch Ltd
76 Dean Street
London W1V 5HA

www.vci.co.uk

A catalogue record for this title is available from the British Library

ISBN 0 233 99746 6

Typeset in Liverpool by Derek Doyle & Associates
Printed in the UK by Mackays of Chatham plc, Chatham, Kent

Contents

Introduction

I can only begin this preamble by humbly seeking pardon in retrospect from the shade of John Nyren, the first and most admirable of cricket writers, for presuming to borrow almost exactly the title of the first and most distinguished of cricket books. Nyren sketched *the* cricketers of his time, the Hambledon pantheon in immortal prose: there they all are, Silver Billy Beldam, James Aylward, poor Noah Mann, the Walkers, those anointed clod-stumpers, David Harris, John Small and his violin and Harry Hall, the gingberbread baker from Farnham. My title has no definite article since over the years the tally of obituaries below my name is now upwards of 120, from which I have here extracted eighty-odd and regret that the notices of many more good men must remain in reserve.

Before I pass on I must congratulate Mr Ashley Mote on discovering in his researches 165 years after it was written the previously unknown manuscript of John Nyren's text as collected and edited by Charles Cowden Clarke and published in 1833, in nine instalments of a weekly magazine called *The Town*. The edition of 1907 edited by E. V. Lucas and entitled *The Hambledon Men* is now hard to come by, and in any case lacks Mr Mote's annotations. The Mote edition, including the text of *The Young Cricketer's Tutor*, which I warmly recommend, was published in 1998 by Robson Books.

Some of my obituaries were first published in *The Cricketer*; the President of which venerable magazine has given himself permission to include them. Most of them, however, were first published in the *Daily Telegraph*, to whose Managing Director, the Hon. Jeremy Deedes, I am deeply indebted for permission to republish (in certain distinguished cases for the second time).

There is, of course, no copyright in a title, as Sir Timothy Rice and I were reminded recently when a publication lifted that of the video made officially by us for MCC, called *Lord's – the Home of Cricket*. Incidentally that felicitous writer, A. A. Thomson, very nearly borrowed Nyren's title when in 1967 he published *Cricketers of My Times*. Come to think of it, I would have had even better grounds than he for making the *Time* plural. The idea of making a book of my obituaries came in fact from the four books of *Daily Telegraph* obituaries which have been so popular, edited by Hugh Montgomery-Massingberd. In most cases he was re-editing notices which had passed through his hands in his years as Obituaries Editor from 1986 to 1994, a date on which he suddenly came perilously close to being a subject on his own page. As it is, he has forsworn daily journalism though not, I am sure, the more relaxed disciplines of authorship. In token of a long and happy association it is a pleasure to dedicate this selection of my notices to him.

Though my association with the *Daily Telegraph* dates only from 1946 and I was batting on an awkward wicket during most of the war years, I decided to remember some more notable casualties. It is therefore true to say that these obituaries cover a period of sixty years from 1940 to the eve of the millennium. Peter Eckersley, the first to go in 1940, was a friend, and the fact is that with all the 80-odd included bar one I was on terms either of acquaintance or friendship. The exception, about whom I heard much but never shook hands with, was one of the greater cricketers, the much-loved George Hirst. As a boy I merely watched him in the first county match I ever saw, between Surrey and Yorkshire at The Oval in August 1919.

On the subject of war casualties I must add that Test cricketers from the other countries were also among the fallen, Ross Gregory of Australia, A. W. Briscoe, C. M. Francois and A. B. C. Langton of South Africa and D. A. R. Moloney of New Zealand. And English casualties did not, of course, end with the seven I have commemorated. Claude Ashton and Roger Winlaw were lost in a tragic air collision over Liverpool. R. P. Nelson and C. W. C. Packe had captained Northants and Leicestershire respectively. Somerset lost John Lee, brother of Harry and Frank, F. M. McRae and the England centre three-quarter R. A. Gerrard. G. D. Kemp-Welch, of Cambridge and Warwickshire, was one of the many killed by the bomb on the Guards chapel. All schools had lengthy Rolls of Honour; of the Eton XIs of the 1930s nearly 20 were lost: 20 Oxford and Cambridge blues perished. Of those in their 'teens or twenties who might have been destined for great things on the cricket field one can only speculate. Small wonder that the early post-war county sides wore an elderly look.

All this will make unfamiliar reading to the average cricket follower of today: for those of a historical bent, however, it may help to explain how Test and county cricket took time to recover from the Second World War, just as they had from the First.

I have divided my subjects for ease of reference into ten compartments which seemed suitable, though obviously many – indeed most – can qualify for a second or even a third category apart from probably being Household Names: for instance Frank Worrell, Walter Robins, Freddy Brown . . . Most cricketers who reach distinction have developed an agreeable philosophy of life, warm in friendship, reasonably modest and, above all, with no shortage of humour. There are misfits, of course, but few who merit Rockley Wilson's severest turn-down: 'only a fairly nice chap really'.

I must underline a few points about what you are about to read, and firstly that the length of the obituary bears only very limited relevance to the reputation of the subject. As every journalist knows on some days there seem to be oceans of space available, on another 'space is very tight, old boy'. It should be borne in mind that facts in the narrative were true at the time of writing, but may have been since overtaken. In places I have re-edited entries to avoid confusion.

The exclusion of a few can be explained by my having covered their exits in the lengthy Commentaries which were required when Sundays in the long ago cricket world were days of rest. Hence the kind comment of the critic who wrote that the prevailing sound on a Monday morning was of Swanton barking up the wrong tree.

I usually enjoy writing obituaries for the opportunity they can provide to recall great deeds and wherever possible to portray something of the man behind his accomplishments. Obituaries can bring a measure of comfort to relations, friends and admirers. To see a man in perspective is often to recollect feats long forgotten. As to basic facts I have thought it best to assemble these in a pro forma at the head of each entry: places and dates of birth and death, schools where it has been possible to ascertain them, teams played for, and career figures both first-class and where applicable in Tests. I am deeply beholden, as all cricket writers must be, to the monumental *Who's Who of Cricketers* containing the basic details of every player who since the dawn of time has appeared in a first-class match in the British Isles – even if he only made a duck or (I believe) if he never batted. Seeing that this invaluable *opus* runs to 1,200 pages it is not surprising that it has been compiled by three devoted men, Philip Bailey, Philip Thorn and Peter Wynne-Thomas. I expect they thought that they could improve on the *Cricket Form at a Glance, 1878–1937,* by Sir Home Gordon, Bart, which the late Bob Arrowsmith used to describe as 'that monumental work of fiction'. These legends have been put together with characteristic care by Mr David Robertson, my fellow Kent CCC curator. I am grateful to him also for general assistance and proof-reading, as also I am to my long-suffering Secretary, Mrs Doreen Waite, who kindly released me from my promise to her that *Last Over* would be my swan-song. Miss Wendy Wimbush has once again compiled a model index.

Out of admiration for Miss Molly Hide and respect for women's cricket in general I am pleased to include the obituary of this fine cricketer and handsome presence who captained England with success in both England and Australia.

I am only too conscious of the fact that I named the book published with David Rayvern Allen three years ago *Last Over* because I firmly intended it to be so. I'm now being told that no one believed me. Nevertheless I'll say it again. The fact is that Tim Forrester, managing director of André Deutsch, and his colleague, Louise Dixon, took to the idea of the book with enthusiasm. I shall hope to repeat the success of an earlier one, copies of which I was bidden to sign by Mr Tommy Joy, for so many years the genial genius of Hatchards.

'You realise you are our Uncle Fred this Christmas?'

'How so?'

'Oh, you know, "What the devil can we get for Uncle Fred?" '

E. W. Swanton
Sandwich August 1999

Statistics Explained

Batting: Matches/Innings/Times not out/Runs/Highest/Average

Bowling: Runs/Wickets/Average

1

THE GOLDEN AGE

S. F. BARNES

Hands of an artist

Barnes, Sydney Francis   Professional

b: Smethwick, Staffordshire, 19 April 1873

Teams: Warwickshire, Lancashire, Wales, MacLaren to Australia,
MCC, England

Career batting:
133-173-50-1573-93-12.78; *ct* 72
Bowling: 12289-719-17.09

Test batting:
27-39-9-242-38*-8.06; *ct* 12
Bowling: 3106-189-16.43

d: Chadsmoor, Staffordshire, 26 December 1967. Aged 94.

Sydney Barnes was perhaps the greatest bowler of all time. In one of his most vivid images Neville Cardus has written of F.R. Spofforth that his bowling 'let in one of the coldest blasts of antagonism that ever blew across a June field'. If there is one man to whom 'The Demon's' countrymen would not have denied a similar tribute, it must surely be Sydney Barnes. Indeed, between the two men there was a striking resemblance: both began as fast bowlers pure and simple, but soon adjusted their pace into a mere reinforcement of their great bowling art: both were tall and wiry, long-armed and strong-fingered: both had something of Cassius's lean and hungry, indeed predatory, look and both commanded alike the physical presence, the personality and the sustained intent to dominate the batsmen opposing them.

Barnes appeared in three matches for Warwickshire in the seasons of 1894–96 with singularly little success. Migrating to the Lancashire League, he still failed to make his mark in the few games which he was given for that county during the seasons 1899–1901. Therefore his selection by A. C. MacLaren for the team which he took to Australia in the winter of 1901–2 was something

1

of a nine days' wonder. But the insight of that judge of cricket was triumphantly justified when in the first two Test matches, Barnes took 19 wickets for 15 apiece; an injury to a knee then put him out of action. There followed two full seasons for Lancashire in which he took a total of 213 wickets, but he then committed himself finally to the Leagues and Staffordshire, emerging into first-class cricket only to play in Test matches and for the Players against the Gentlemen. It says much for the wealth of bowling talent open to the selectors that, though he went to Australia with the side captained by A.O. Jones in 1907–8 and took 24 wickets in the Tests on that tour, he had only played in four Test matches at home when his third visit to Australia with Warner's side in 1911–12 set the decisive seal on his fame. On that tour, with F. R. Foster as his brilliant partner, he took 34 wickets in the five games and was universally acclaimed as the greatest bowler ever to have visited that country. He started the second Test at Melbourne by taking the first four wickets for one run.

Before war came, however, still greater heights were to be scaled: in the three Test matches against the South Africans played in the Triangular Tournament of 1912 he took 34 wickets for eight runs each and then, for the MCC side that toured that country in 1913–14, he took in four Test matches 49 wickets for an average of under 11. His 17 in the Johannesburg match has since been surpassed by Laker's feat at Manchester, but no other bowler in history has averaged 12 wickets a match in a Test series nor can any man rival his figures in Test cricket, and that against our strongest opponents, of 189 wickets at a cost of 16.43 each.

After the war he played in only some half-dozen first-class matches, but for Wales against the West Indies in 1928 his analysis was 12 for 118 and in the next year against the South Africans he took 18 of their wickets in two matches for 7 each; he was then 56. With such achievements on the highest level it is small wonder that his record for Staffordshire and in the Leagues verges on the fantastic; for the former in 20 seasons he took over 1,400 wickets at a cost of 8 each, while in the League his bag was something of the order of 3,700 for less than 7 each.

Barnes was a good enough batsman to score over 30 against the Gentlemen at Lord's and with 38 not out to play a decisive part in the only Test victory gained by Jones's side in Australia. Had Barnes been born 50 years later how would he have appeared in action on the television screen to the millions for whom his name would have been a household word? Two steps and then a few long springy strides, a long arm swinging high over and past an intensely concentrated face, and then the final whip from wrist and fingers of steel; the pace would be lively and variable, the length superbly controlled: above all there would be a dominating impression of sustained hostility directed by a calculating mind.

A typical over: first, perhaps, two very late out-swingers straight enough and well enough up to force the batsman to play off the front foot, then two penetrating off-breaks, the fifth ball a fast leg-break – and a leg-break it was rather than a leg-cutter – and finally such a delivery as on his great Australian tour clean bowled Victor Trumper at the height of his powers, a ball swerving from the leg stump on to the off and then breaking back to hit the leg. 'It was the sort of ball', said Charlie Macartney, 'that a man might see when he was tight.'

Meeting him in old age, I was fascinated by those large, strong, sensitive hands. In his eighties he was employed by Staffordshire County Council for his calligraphy.

C. B. FRY

All-rounder deluxe

Fry, Charles Burgess   Amateur

b. West Croydon, Surrey, 25 April 1872

School: Repton   Teams: Oxford U. Sussex, London County,
                              Hampshire, Hawke to South Africa,
                              India, England.

Career batting:
394–658–43–30886–258*–50.22; 94 hundreds; ct. 240
Bowling: 4872–166–29.34

Test batting:
26–41–3–1223–144–32.18; 2 hundreds; ct. 17
Bowling: 3–0

d. Child's Hill, Hampstead, 7 September 1956.   Aged 84

Charles Fry – classical scholar, diplomat, trainer of youth, school-master, author, etcetera – attracted sporting superlatives to a degree beyond the rest of mankind. He was eminent from his Repton days first as a footballer, then as an athlete and cricketer. He reached a Cup Final with Southampton and as an original Corinthian played soccer for England. As an all-round athlete he shared a world record in the long jump. At Oxford he captained the University simultaneously at cricket, soccer and athletics. He played rugby football on the wing for the University all one season and only missed a fourth blue because of injury.

He played first in a Test match at the age of 23 and was selected for England (though he did not play) when 49. He wrote a treatise on batsmanship and put theory into practice by scoring more than 30,000 runs with an average of 50. He made history by scoring six hundreds in a row. His partnerships for Sussex with his great friend 'Ranji' were legendary, unique alike in size and style.

Neville Cardus thought him 'a great Englishman, measured by any standards'. To John Arlott he was 'a most incredible man'. John Woodcock rated him 'a figure of truly heroic stature'. On my estimation he was 'surely the finest all-rounder of his own or any age'.

Yet there were aspects of Fry's life as disclosed in a recent biography by Iain Wilton, and in a book about his dreadful wife entitled *The Captain's Lady* by Ronald Morris, which blur the heroic image. When Wilton set out to write *C.B. Fry*, the sub-title *An English Hero* no doubt reflected the subject he had in mind. However his researches revealed a picture different in important ways from Fry's autobiography *Life Worth Living* which for many years – it was first published in 1939 – was accepted as gospel. His sporting career was after all well documented, and it told a story of high and astonishingly diverse achievement. There are aspects which Fry records in a self-deprecating way. In parts, however, he has been economical with the truth, and there were phases of his life which he simply ignored.

He writes of his attempts to foster Anglo-German friendship in the 1930s. Hence his admiration for Ribbentrop and the scoop of an interview with Hitler, by whom he was naïvely impressed. The Führer assured him that there was nothing at all militaristic about the nationwide Nazi Youth Movement. His political inclinations were on this evidence firmly to the right when *Live Worth Living* was published in 1939. He had however fought three elections as a Liberal in the early 1920s. They were unsuccessful and the book makes no mention of them.

He writes of his command of the training ship HMS *Mercury*, anchored on the Hamble river near Southampton, as his life's work. But was it? The ship had been bought and set up by Charles Hoare, a rich member of the banking family in the 1880s as a training school for the Royal and Merchant Navies. Hoare had left his wife and lived openly with a vivacious and attractive young woman, Beatrice Sumner, by whom he had two children. Hoare showed a benevolent interest in the *Mercury* and encouraged Fry to do so. The latter was attracted by 'Beatie' whom Hoare encouraged to interest herself in the running of the ship.

Fry, on coming down from Oxford, taught for two years at Charterhouse, before suddenly giving that up and to the astonishment of the sporting world marrying Hoare's mistress. The unholy triangle persisted, the Frys being financed by Hoare, who was thought to be the father of a daughter, Charis, officially Fry's offspring. When in 1908 Hoare died, Charles Fry worked with success to establish the *Mercury* as a charitable trust, with himself as titular head. He however had been for the previous decade a full-time cricketer, by now a Test batsman of legendary fame, playing firstly for Sussex and latterly with Hampshire.

The running of the *Mercury* devolved largely on Beatie, who established a brutal regime of beating by petty officers, the culprits, even twelve-year-olds, being tied down to receive their punishment. There was also, according to Morris, a system whereby offenders were obliged to fight against much stronger boys while Beatie sat at the ring-side shouting, 'Make him bleed, boy! Make him bleed.' If these things are hard to credit the character of Charles Fry's wife is portrayed at first hand by her daughter-in-law, Yvonne, the widow of his son Stephen. According to Wilton, who interviewed her in 1997, she was 'a domineering creature', 'an awful woman' and 'terrible', adding that Stephen had been reluctant to introduce her to his mother until the last possible moment, in case she found the experience too off-putting. Moreover, the lady who married Beatrice's other son, Robin Hoare, admitted she would never have done so if she had met her prospective mother-in-law before the wedding.

The extent to which what went on in the training ship was known to C. B. can never be established. During the First World War he was given honorary title of Commander. But when the war ended it was his wife who in the 1918 Birthday Honours was summoned to Buckingham Palace to receive the OBE for services in the training of young seamen. Fry moved in more glamorous circles before the war – he met the literary world as the editor of *C. B. Fry's Magazine*, for instance. Nevertheless the responsibility for the *Mercury* was his, and if he did not know the half of it he should have done; Fry's own treatment of the boys according to 'old boys' was uniformly fair and amiable.

After the war, acting as a sort of ADC and companion to Ranji he took part in this capacity at the League of Nations at Geneva, For Ranji had succeeded to the throne of his home state, becoming the Maharaja Jam Saheb of Nawanagar. He entertained in princely style, C.B. basking in his reflected glory. Hence the legendary story of how he might have become the King of Albania. Albania, having gained entry to the League, were apparently looking for an English country gentleman with an income of, say, £10,000 a year to occupy their vacant throne. There was some parleying with an Albanian delegation including a Bishop who, Fry thought, bore a singular likeness to W. G. Grace. However the Jam Saheb, realising that he would be touched for the annual £10,000 and would also be deprived of Fry's services, called the thing off.

The remaining episode of Fry's life concerning which he was, understandably for his times, completely reticent was the mental illness which first occurred during his last year at Oxford and, more seriously and for a much more lengthy period, from 1928 to the end of 1933. By the autumn of 1894 Fry had touched a pinnacle of such acclaim as no undergraduate had ever aspired to. He had led the University to victory over Cambridge at cricket, soccer and athletics. He had the looks of a Greek god. 'He stepped straight out of the frieze of the Parthenon,' according to H. S. Altham. He made a hundred at Lord's and took a First in Classical Moderations. Never a shy man, he adorned the social scene. What then? Whatever the contributory causes – the serious illness of his mother may have been one, his parents' poverty and his rising debts perhaps another – suddenly deep depression took over. In 'Greats' he scraped only a Fourth, at Lord's he made 0 and 1. His confidence was only gradually restored by an invitation from Lord Hawke (always thereafter his strong supporter) to accompany his team to South Africa.

As to the second malady, the cause may well have been at least exacerbated by his marriage. When his great contemporary and friend F. E. Smith (Lord Birkenhead) at Hamble said that surely his work there had been for him a backwater, Fry asked whether it was not best to be happy. But must there not have been deep differences between him and the woman Beatie had become? Stephen Fry put it succinctly, 'My mother ruined my father's life.' It may not have been a coincidence that whereas Ranji had footed the bills for Fry's comfortable seclusion his reappearance followed closely on the death of his benefactor.

When Charles emerged from his years of seclusion his spirits were as buoyant and his mind as keen as could be imagined. His *Evening Standard* column first burst upon the world on 2 May 1934, this being the first day of the Australian tour which as usual opened at Worcester. We sat together, I writing the straight report of the match for the sports pages while he was embarked for the first time on 'C. B. Fry says.' Illustrated by the author's head complete with monocle, the feature was at once promoted by the Editor, Percy Cudlipp, to the front page.

Fry wrote swiftly on flimsy octavo sheets, talking freely and refreshing himself and his neighbours now and then (including me) with champagne and a sandwich or two provided by his chauffeur and man of many parts, Brooks by name. We were in the front row of the very low New Road stand, within reach of Brooks, plus hamper, on the footpath.

Fry's voice and appearance were alike singular, the one mellifluous, the latter striking to a degree. His jacket was Norfolk in cut with vast side pockets. There depended alongside his Harlequin tie the broad silk ribbon with monocle attached. There would be a waistcoat of contrasting colour. The trousers were unusual in that they ended buttoned above the ankle. If there were a hat it would be broad-brimmed sombrero style. Thus attired, Charles followed the Australians' early matches, with special attention, of course, to Don Bradman. ('The Don is at his Donniest today.')

Charles was unfailingly kind to me, as he also was many years later in contributing a brilliant prologue and epilogue when the *Daily Telegraph* published my reports of the 1954–55 tour of Australia which resulted in Len Hutton retaining the Ashes.

Fry's cricket reflected the man in that, as Altham wrote in *Barclay's World of Cricket*, it 'never revealed itself as an art but rather in the scientific exposition of technique.' His method was built around the theory, 'play back or drive'. The bowler saw a good deal of the bat-maker's name. He made more runs on the on-side than his contemporaries. When set his wicket was the hardest possible to get. Of his 94 hundreds no fewer than 16 were double hundreds.

He reached his peak in 1901 in which season he made 3,147 runs with an average of 78. Whereas his career average was 50 his Test figure was only 32 over a span of 26 matches. As a Test selector and player in 1909 and 1912 he finished strongly. Offered the captaincy of England for the First Test only by Lord Harris in 1912, Fry stipulated all or none and led England to success in the only Triangular series involving Australia and South Africa. His two Test hundreds at the Oval in 1905 and 1907, were of the utmost value. It will be noticed that he took 166 wickets. His action was highly suspect and after being no-balled several times, he never bowled again.

Fry was strong meat for his Edwardian contemporaries and his relationships did not always run smoothly. There were admirers and detractors. It was significant that he was never elected to the MCC committee, let alone being made president. Happily there is today a Charles Fry on the Committee giving service to the Club, his grandson, who also played for Oxford and Hampshire.

GEORGE GUNN

His bat as a walking stick

Gunn, George   Professional

b: Hucknall Torkard, Nottinghamshire, 13 June 1879

Sch: Berridge Road, Nottingham   *Teams:* Nottinghamshire,
                                         MCC, England

Career batting:
643-1061-82-35208-220-35.96; hundreds 62-*ct* 473
Bowling: 2355-66-35.68

Test batting:
15-29-1-1120-122*-40.00; hundreds 2-*ct* 15
Bowling: 8-0

d: Tylers Green, Cuckfield, Sussex, 29 June 1958. Aged 79.

Cricket has always been rich in 'characters' – and they have rarely come richer than the inimitable George Gunn of Nottinghamshire. Devotees of the romantic school of cricket writers, Cardus and Robertson-Glasgow, for instance, will have read word-pictures of this singular son of Notts, nephew of William, brother of John, and father of George Vernon. He was what in the days of Hambledon might have been dubbed a Nonsuch.

I saw him play only when he was nearly finishing, but in his early fifties he was still using the pitch as a sort of promenade, with his bat, so to speak, as a walking-stick.

One of the old touring photographs shows him in a straw hat, and if he had batted in one it would have been in character, perched at a tilt. For he cocked a metaphorical snook at all bowlers, especially the fastest of them.

Perhaps the most extraordinary of all selectorial omissions centred round him. Thirty cricketers – yes, 30 – played for England against Australia in the five Tests of 1921, but Gunn was not asked. In the absence of Hobbs and with the exception of Woolley he looks, retrospectively, just about the first pick among the batsmen. One thing is certain. The omission would not have worried him. Nothing did. He took everything as it came, including going out nearly ten years later with MCC to West Indies, and at the age of 50 averaging 40-odd, in those islands in the sun, against the pace of Griffith, Francis and Constantine.

It had been 22 years since he was first recruited on the spot to reinforce MCC's 1907–8 tour of Australia where he had gone to cure a lung disorder. Though he hit two Test hundreds, one on his first appearance, and topped the averages with 51 and played equally well four years later in Australia in the side which brought back the Ashes, he was chosen only once for a Test in England.

One could only assume that the man who when reproved by his captain for getting out to a poor stroke merely answered 'too 'ot', lost the votes in favour of more conventional alternatives. It might have been different if there had been a stack of runs behind him; but he was selective in his run-getting, which had little to do with the quality of the opposing bowler. He was perhaps more likely to shine against the best rather than the second-best. He and 'Dodge' Whysall made 40 hundreds together for the first wicket, but he chose Andrew Sandham and the grilling heat of Jamaica to put up his most bizarre performance, an opening stand of 332.

'Crusoe' began his *Cricket Prints* with this comment: 'Cricket is still scratching its head about George Gunn, Senior; and it will not readily recover from him. Technically, he was a genius. Aware and capable of orthodoxy, he mostly preferred to laugh at the book of words.'

GEORGE HIRST
Yorkshire personified

Hirst, George Herbert   Professional

b: Kirkheaton, Yorkshire, 7 September 1871

Teams: Yorkshire, Europeans, MCC, England, Stoddart to Australia

Career batting:
826-1217-152-36356-341-34.13; hundreds 60-*ct* 604
Bowling: 51372-2742-18.73

Test batting:
24-38-3-790-85-22.57; *ct* 18
Bowling: 1770-59-30.00

d: Lindley, Huddersfield, Yorkshire, 10 May 1954. Aged 82.

George Hirst, the former Yorkshire and England cricketer, was one of the outstanding all-rounders in the history of the game. His figures attest his greatness as a county cricketer, and if his Test record is modest he at least played a heroic part in the famous Test Match at The Oval in 1902 wherein he and Wilfred Rhodes scored the 15 runs which brought England to victory by one wicket.

There was a gentle steadfastness, and yet at times a clear outspokenness, about Hirst that proclaimed his honesty and integrity. There was surrounding him a quality that made him equally beloved at Eton, where he taught the game for 18 seasons, retiring in 1938, and with equally good effect among the young men from mine and mill who came, spring after spring, to the Yorkshire nets to try their skill for the county of their birth.

Hirst was in at the first real flowering of Yorkshire cricket. In the early 1890s Surrey were supreme. The Yorkshire elevens, for all their native talent, were not much better than a crowd of ill-disciplined roisterers. Lord Hawke's assumption of the captaincy coincided with the arrival of Hirst, Brown and Tunnicliffe. In the ten years from 1893 Yorkshire won the championship six times, and it is true to say that from that moment Yorkshire cricket has seldom looked back. Hirst was an integral member of the side, and of most England elevens intervening, at any rate on English wickets, until after the First World War. He achieved the cricketer's double of 1,000 runs and 100 wickets eleven times. Three times he scored 2,000 runs in a season, and once, in his crowning year of 1906, he scored 2,385 and took 208 wickets. That is an all-round feat that has never been approached.

His speciality as a bowler was a fastish left-arm in-swerve, described by one of his victims as being 'as though one was thrown out from cover-point'. Those who lament the change in the law in respect of the new ball may be reminded that in Hirst's day there was only one new ball per innings. Stories cluster round a man held in wide affection. The one of his comment to Wilfred Rhodes as the latter joined him for the last wicket in the famous Test against Australia at The Oval in 1902, 'We'll get 'em in singles', is plainly apocryphal. A Yorkshireman, if he made any such remark, would have said that they'd get 'em in 'wuns'. But the idea of grafting for victory without heroics is, of course, completely in character.

When a young Eton captain, a much better batsman than bowler, sought to obtain from him a post-mortem on a defeat, all he got was, 'Ye bowled too long, and ye bowled too bad.' But he knew, as did all who ever met George Hirst, that it was the plain talk of a man whose soul was in cricket, and who knew no deceit.

WILFRED RHODES

Records unrepeatable

Rhodes, Wilfred   Professional

b: Kirkheaton, Yorkshire, 29 October 1877

Sch: Hopton National   *Teams:* Yorkshire, Patiala, Europeans,
                                        MCC, England

Career batting:
1110-1534-237-39969-267*-30.81; hundreds 58-*ct* 765
Bowling: 70322-4187-16.72

Test batting:
58-98-21-2325-179-30.19; hundreds 2-*ct* 60
Bowling: 3425-127-26.96

d: Branksome Park, Dorset, 8 July 1973. Aged 95.

In the apostolic succession of left-handed slow bowlers who
have won so many championships for Yorkshire, Wilfred
Rhodes was the third and the greatest; he was, indeed, the classic
exemplar of this always fascinating and challenging cricket art. It
may, too, be a matter for argument whether he or his close friend
and contemporary, George Hirst, was the greatest of Yorkshire
cricketers. Hirst's advocates can still quote his prodigious and,
patently in these days, unrepeatable record of 2,000 runs and 200
wickets in the single season of 1906. To Rhodes, too, however,
belong records that as yet defy comparisons: his total capture of
wickets, 4,187 for 16 each; his 16 'doubles' of over a thousand runs
and a hundred wickets in a season; his 2,325 runs and 127 wickets
for England in Test matches – and that, be it remembered, before
every summer and almost every winter brought its Tests. But perhaps even these scarcely challenge the imagination more than the
memory of his return to the England side in 1926, 27 years since
he had first played for it, to bowl Australia out at The Oval in the
match that at long last regained for us the Ashes.

As a batsman alone he would have been sure of his niche in history. Though originally played purely for his bowling, he soon showed that he could also bat, and it was much less of a surprise to Yorkshiremen than to others when in the first Test of the 1903–4 Australian tour he helped R. E. Foster in a last-wicket partnership of 130, and when the former's glorious 287 ended was left undefeated with 40 to his name. Two summers later he scored 1,580 runs and, with 182 wickets, had his greatest all-round season. In the winter of 1911–12 he returned to Australia to go in first for England with Jack Hobbs: at Melbourne they made history in what is still the highest opening stand for England in a Test match, 323, a partnership memorable not only for the mastery of their batting but for the combined enterprise and security of their running between the wickets.

As a batsman Rhodes was a craftsman rather than an artist; with a pronouncedly two-shouldered open stance he scored the majority of his runs on the on-side, though he could steer his off-drives and cuts with effective precision. If the range of his technique was limited, it was directed by the shrewdest of heads and sustained by the most tenacious of wills; he liked batting and it was up to the opposition to get him out. His highest score was 267 not out, against Leicestershire in 1921 – clearly not too old at 44!

Coming into the Yorkshire side in 1898, he established himself immediately and decisively, taking 13 wickets in his first county match. In the first three years of this century he took 725 wickets for 14 apiece and in his first Test match, against Australia at Birmingham in 1902, when they were bowled out for 36, his analysis was seven for 17. If his figures of six for 4 in dismissing Notts for 13 in the previous summer and five for 6 against Victoria on his first Australian tour are even more sensational, neither, in the quality of opposition, can compare with his 15 for 124 which won the Melbourne Test match in 1903–4.

In the Tests of that tour he took 31 wickets, a record unparalleled by any bowler of his type. In the years immediately preceding the first World War his bowling, though still very much of a force, took second place to his batting, but on the resumption of the game in 1919 and with Drake and Booth both killed, he found himself called upon to shoulder once more the double role. He was now in his 43rd year yet in nine out of the next eleven seasons he achieved 'the double.'

Where, then, lay the secret of his bowling greatness? He had, of course, a beautifully controlled, economical and rhythmical action which ensured supreme accuracy of length and direction. He was a master of the stock left-hander's spin and could vary it with the ball that came on with his arm, but above all he was supreme in the art of studying the individual batsman and inducing him to play the wrong stroke by sinuous and elusive variations of flight. If, as has been said, Mailey bowled like a millionaire and Grimmett like a miser, Rhodes was the hardheaded financier, ready to buy his wickets but never at an extravagant price. And how often, in those far-off days of handsome driving, was the price of a four or two from inviting half-volleys and then 'caught Denton bowled Rhodes' at straight long-off? 'Where is his field?' he was wont to ask of a slow bowler when in the later years of his blindness he would sit 'listening in' at some great match; and when he heard that there was no man out, he would murmur, 'He's bowling bad.'

On his retirement in 1929, Rhodes went as coach to Harrow School but whereas Hirst was such a success at Eton, Rhodes found it more difficult to convey his talents to schoolboys. He left Harrow in 1936, and after the war his eyesight deteriorated. For many years he was totally blind, but he continued to attend and follow the home Test matches almost to the end and his judgment on the game remained as shrewd as ever.

A great English cricketer, he was above all a Yorkshireman; his blue eyes and fresh complexion might suggest the Pennine moors but there was a vein of iron in his cricket soul.

REGGIE SPOONER
Style and elegance

Spooner, Reginald Herbert   Amateur

b: Litherland, Lancashire, 21 October 1880

Sch: Marlborough   *Teams:* Lancashire, MCC, England

Career batting:
237-393-16-13681-247-36.28; hundreds 31-*ct* 142
Bowling: 582-6-97.00

Test batting:
10-15-0-481-119-32.06; hundreds 1-*ct* 4

d: Lincoln, 2 October 1961. Aged 80.

R. H. Spooner, the England and Lancashire cricketer, was the last survivor of that classical school of English batsmen who held spectators entranced in what has since come to be called The Golden Age. MacLaren, Fry, Ranji, J. T. Tyldesley, Jessop, Jackson, R. E. Foster, Spooner: they were the names to conjure with after W. G. had thrown down his bat at last and Hobbs and Woolley were still on the threshold of greatness. In terms of runs and hundreds some of these must be accounted Spooner's superiors; but, as Cardus would say, one does not measure Mozart by the number of his crotchets and quavers. In purity and charm of style I cannot think (though, alas! I write only from assimilated knowledge) that anyone, not even Lionel Palairet, can have ranked above him.

Spooner was tall and slim, and the wrist of the rackets player gave a sheen and a rhythm to all his strokes. His off-driving especially was a thing of joy, and in the days when the first three names on Lancashire's order were those of himself, MacLaren and Tyldesley, there was no better play anywhere than was to be seen at Old Trafford. His ability did not end with his batting for, as might have been expected of a talented all-round player of games, he was numbered among the classic cover points.

16

Spooner had a wonderful record at Marlborough, where from 1896 to 1899 he excelled in every variety of sport, rugby football, hockey, fives, rackets and athletics as well as cricket. In 1898 an innings of 139 against Rugby at Lord's showed that here was a schoolboy of something more than promise and when the next year at Lord's he made 69 and 198 in the annual match he set everyone talking about him. A fortnight later against Middlesex on the same ground he made his first appearance for Lancashire and scored 44 and 83, his play against Albert Trott being remarkable for its maturity as well as its style.

With a commission in the Manchester Regiment he went to the South African war and could play no more cricket until 1903. Altogether he made 25 centuries for Lancashire, his highest score being 247 against Notts in 1903, when also he and MacLaren put on 368 for the first wicket against Gloucestershire, a Lancashire record to this day. Spooner played ten times for England in this country, seven against Australia and three against South Africa, off whose bowlers, in the Lord's match of the 1912 Triangular Tournament, he made 119. One of the greatest innings he ever played was his 114 for the Gentlemen on a fiery Lord's pitch in the historic match of 1906 when Fielder took all 10 wickets, when H. Martyn stood up to the fast bowling of Brearley and Knox, when Jessop did some wonderful hitting and the Gentlemen won by 45 runs.

During the Great War he served with the Lincolnshire Regiment, was wounded at La Bassée and at Hooge, and was never quite the same player afterwards. He accepted to captain MCC in Australia in 1920–21 but because of injury he had to withdraw in favour of J. W. H. T. Douglas, and first-class cricket saw little of him afterwards. Thus like many other famous amateurs, Jackson, Fry, L. C. H. Palairet and C. L. Townsend among them, he never went to Australia.

Spooner had the distinction of being one of the select few who have played for England at rugby football as well as cricket – A. N. Hornby, F. Mitchell, S. M. J. Woods, A. E. Stoddart and M. J. K. Smith are the others – but in the early years of the century English rugger was suffering from the 'Northern Split' over Broken Time, and on his one appearance in 1903 Wales at Swansea won another of a long string of victories. He was a fine rider to hounds and a first-rate shot. Visitors to Woodhall Spa for golf and cricket in later years will remember him as a gentle person, modest in his talk, which had in it an echo of the charm that characterised his cricket.

SIR PELHAM WARNER

A life totally involved

Warner, Sir Pelham Francis   Amateur

b: The Hall, Port of Spain, Trinidad, 2 October 1873

Sch: Rugby   *Teams:* Oxford U., Middlesex, MCC, England,
                  Hawke to West Indies, South Africa, Australia
                  and New Zealand, Warner to North America

Career batting:
519-875-75-29028-244-36.28; hundreds 60-*ct* 183
Bowling: 636-15-42.40

Test batting: 15-28-2-622-132*-23.92; hundreds 1-*ct* 3

d: West Lavington, Sussex, 30 January 1963. Aged 89.

Few men, arguably none, have had a longer or a wider influence on cricket than the man who was universally known as 'Plum' Warner. He was successively or in combination Test captain, Test selector, manager, author and journalist. Without aspiring to stand among the greatest, as a batsman he was good enough to be chosen for England at the height of The Golden Age. As captain of the first MCC side to Australia in 1903–4, he won back the Ashes which had eluded England for the last four rubbers. In 1911–12 he was again chosen to take MCC to Australia and again he won back the Ashes. His influence with the side was clearly, as ever, a great asset, but after the first match of the tour at Adelaide, where he began with an innings of 161 against South Australia, his health broke down so badly that he was confined for six weeks to a nursing home, and did not play again on the tour. However, a young England side with five men under 25, led by J. W. H. T. Douglas, beat Australia by four Tests to one.

England's opening bowlers, Barnes and F. R. Foster, took 66 wickets between them. This was the series which saw Barnes at his best. He began the Second Test at Melbourne by taking the first four

18

Australian wickets for one run in five overs. This side of 1911–12 was among England's best ever. Warner led Middlesex from 1908 until 1920, in which year, amid a wealth of sentiment, just short of his 47th birthday, they won the County Championship.

In 1932–33 Warner was joint-manager of what became known as the Bodyline tour. He was captain of an MCC side to South America at the age of 54. He had been first appointed to the MCC Committee in 1904 and served on it for the best part of sixty years. He was nominated President in 1950–51, and later became the first-ever Life Vice-President.

In 1921 he founded *The Cricketer* and was its editor until the war. He also began thirteen years as Cricket Correspondent of *The Morning Post*. He was already the author of several books, and he continued to write about the game in a facile, pleasant and always diplomatic manner up to and even after the war. What seems extraordinary today is that he served without serious demur and simultaneously as Chairman of the Selectors in 1926, 1931–2 and 1935–8 without giving up his journalism. In fact from his own writings Plum's life in cricket was copiously recorded from childhood days in Trinidad (where his father was Attorney-General) through Rugby and Oxford to an absorption in the game to which there is scarcely a parallel. The only barrier to his pursuit of cricket was its strain on his health. He was a slight figure, not constitutionally strong.

Captain of the Rugby XI for two years, he did not win his Oxford blue until his third year. He was not a particularly gifted batsman, but he was a dedicated, determined one lucky enough to have attracted on first coming down from the University the attention of that Odysseus of cricket, Lord Hawke. He was called to the Bar (though he never practised) in 1896 and the following year, having made something of a mark with Middlesex, received from Hawke the invitation to go as a member of his side to the West Indies. That was the start of a friendship which, so far as Plum Warner was concerned, was invaluable.

For countless years the Lords Harris and Hawke were the dominant figures on the MCC Committee, and when the club at last decided to take responsibility for an official tour to Australia there is little doubt that, after F. S. Jackson had declined the invitation, one lord if not both made the decision in Warner's favour. As a leader, especially of a touring side, he earned full marks all round. He was solicitude itself to all under his command both on the field and off. He was a good tactician. Both amateurs and professionals enjoyed playing under him and gave of their best. The more famous figure overlooked by MCC was A. C. MacLaren, a high-class batsman and reputedly a great theorist who, however, had lost the last three rubbers to Joe Darling of Australia by an aggregate of seven Tests to two.

Warner, then, whose Test experience only comprised two Tests in South Africa, took to Australia a side lacking four household names in MacLaren, Fry, Ranji and Jackson. He had, however, two young men of the highest promise in R. E. Foster and B. J. T. Bosanquet, the inventor of the googly, and each had leading parts to play. England regained the Ashes by winning three of the first four Tests before losing the last, the captain going in first with Tom Hayward and averaging 27.

He laid down a pattern then for touring cricketers on the field and off it which has been followed with varying success ever since. No one had a deeper sense of what tours abroad should imply. Warner's reputation as a captain was secure.

Warner took over the Middlesex captaincy in 1908 until the war, and they were up with the leaders annually. He joined the Inns of Court as a Territorial, was seconded to the War Office and in 1916 was discharged in the rank of Captain. He nevertheless carried on playing in 1919, and in 1920 Middlesex won a great duel against Surrey at Lord's to take the Championship. Plum, wearing his favourite Harlequin cap, was carried shoulder-high from the field: a grandstand finish if ever there was one.

Warner seized every chance to promote cricket. Throughout the First War there was no play at Lord's. At the start of the Second War, as acting Secretary of MCC he encouraged as much cricket as possible, and many a hard-pressed citizen and serviceman on leave passed through the turnstiles.

As a selector he had one weakness, the more surprising in view of his own brand of captaincy. His contemporaries never thought of Jardine as a leader. Did not Rockley Wilson, his cricket master at Winchester, say on hearing of Jardine's appointment, 'Well, we shall win the Ashes, but we may lose a Dominion'? Equally, very few of Walter Hammond's contemporaries would have seen in him the essentials of captaincy, especially of a touring side. Plum's love of cricket was of benefit in several directions; but his complete failure to influence Jardine as his manager in 1932–33 was a bitter memory for the rest of his life.

2
BETWEEN TWO WARS

BILL BOWES

Half of a winning pair

Bowes, William Eric   Professional

b: Elland, Yorkshire, 25 July 1908

Sch: Armley Park Council School   *Teams:* Yorkshire, MCC, England

Career batting:
372-326-148-1528-43*-8.58; *ct* 138
Bowling: 27470-1639-16.76

Test batting:
15-11-5-28-10*-4.66; *ct* 2
Bowling: 1519-68-22.33

d: Otley, Yorkshire, 4 September 1987. Aged 79.

Bill Bowes's name will be always associated with that of Hedley Verity: a sufficiency of speed at one end, of spin at the other, and artistry and guile at both. Although born in the heart of the West Riding, Bowes came to first-class cricket not through the Yorkshire system but as a member of the Lord's staff which he joined in answer to an advertisement. Elderly MCC members may recall a very tall, somewhat shambling youth looking anything but a budding bowler wearing pince-nez secured to his ear by a chain. Bowes first came to notice by taking a hat-trick against Cambridge in his second first-class match. Yorkshire soon claimed their own, MCC releasing him from a nine-year contract. From 1931 to 1939 Bowes took 100 wickets a season, soon subordinating sheer pace and an over-emphasis on the bouncer in favour of skilful use of the seam. He bowled from his height of 6ft 4in with an arm at full upward stretch, generally to a full length with a late outswing and life and lift on almost any pitch.

Under Brian Sellers's tight leadership, with Verity in support and nowt given away in the field, Bowes was the finest county opening bowler of his generation. In the field his mobility was modest, and as a batsman, though dogged at a pinch, he goes down to history as one of the few who have taken more wickets (1,639 at 17 apiece) than they have made runs (1,528, average 8).

In the winter of 1932–33 Bowes went to Australia as the fourth fast bowler on what became the 'Bodyline tour,' and is remembered for bowling Bradman for a duck first ball at Melbourne when the Don dragged the expected bouncer on to his stumps. That was Bowes's only wicket and his only Test of the series. Very much a bowler for English conditions, Bowes took 68 Test wickets at 22 runs a time – an economical rate considering he saw so much of Bradman, whose wicket he took four times more, albeit after he had made big scores. At the age of 40 Bowes settled down to a long career of cricket writing. He was an acknowledged authority on bowling theory and in much demand as a coach. His dry humour enlivened many a press box, and as a member of the Magic Circle he could occasionally be induced to surprise his friends with his skill as a conjuror.

FRANK CHESTER

Set new standards

Chester, Frank   Professional

b: Bushey, Hertfordshire, 20 January 1895

Teams: Worcestershire

Career batting:
55-92-18-1771-178*-23.95; hundreds 4-*ct* 25
Bowling: 2561-81-31.61

d: Bushey, Hertfordshire, 8 April 1957. Aged 62.

The news of Frank Chester's death came as a shock to the cricket world, for there had been no intimation he was seriously ill. But his health had been bad for a long time, and it was this that caused his retirement from umpiring at the end of the 1955 season when still just short of his 60th birthday. Chester was by common agreement the best of all umpires, and furthermore one whose ability raised the whole standard and standing of his craft. But his personality, which communicated itself unfailingly to the crowds, and the story of cricketing promise cut short which led to his becoming an umpire, combined to make the man a sporting institution.

On the recommendation of Alec Hearne, Chester, at the age of 14, went to qualify for Worcestershire. At 16 and a half he won his county cap and by the time the Great War came after less than three full seasons' play he was acclaimed an England cricketer in embryo. As a bowler he was an exponent of both sorts of spin, as a batsman a free stroke-maker who in an innings of 178 not out against Essex hit the late 'Johnny' Douglas (then just about the best opening bowler in England) for four sixes.

Having survived the second battle of Loos, Chester was transferred to Salonika where, when guarding ammunition, he was hit in the arm by a piece of shrapnel. Penicillin being then unknown, he endured various operations and ultimately amputation. He began his first-class umpiring in 1922 at the age of 26, and made his mark so rapidly that two years later he was standing in a Test match. In all he stood in 48 Tests, and for 28 years as an umpire. He described the three chief requisites of an umpire as 'hearing, eyesight and knowledge of the laws'. But that leaves out of account concentration and strength of character, both of which Chester commanded in full measure, and also something intangible which Ronny Aird perhaps expressed when, on hearing the news yesterday, he said: 'He was an inspiration to other umpires. He seemed to have a flair for the job, and did the right thing by instinct.'

The best epitaph to his skill comes from the greatest of all modern cricketers, Sir Donald Bradman: 'Without hesitation I rank Frank Chester as the greatest umpire under whom I played. In my four seasons' cricket in England he stood for the large percentage of the matches and seldom made a mistake. On the other hand, he gave some really wonderful decisions. Not only was his judgment sound, but Chester exercised a measure of control over the game which I think was desirable.'

Latterly, before he gave in to persistent ill-health, Chester now and then fell into mortal error, and he neither appreciated, nor was appreciated, by the 1953 Australians, who were irked by his apparently dictatorial manner. But he often umpired when he should have been in bed. Until the last few years he was as nearly infallible as a man could be in his profession, and by his conscientiousness and zeal served as an example to all.

LEONARD CRAWLEY

Perfectionist all round

Crawley, Leonard George   Amateur

b: Nacton, Suffolk, 26 July 1903

Sch: Harrow   *Teams:* Worcestershire, Essex, Cambridge U., MCC

Career batting:
109-177-9-5227-222-31.11; hundreds 8-*ct* 42
Bowling: 57-0

d: Worlington, Suffolk, 9 July 1981. Aged 77.

Leonard Crawley was the most distinguished sporting member of a remarkable family – an outstanding all-round games player, who grew up in the vintage amateur period directly after the First World War. Though cricket perhaps was his first love, it was as golf correspondent of the *Daily Telegraph*, and – for quite a while coincidentally – a leading golfer that he will chiefly be remembered. A year after he joined the paper in 1946 he was still playing top for Great Britain in the Walker Cup, and many of his 97 international appearances lay ahead. He played four times in the Walker Cup between 1932 and 1947, and was four times winner of the President's Putter. He won the English Championship at 27, when he was better known as a cricketer, and was twice runner-up. He twice won the Worplesdon Foursomes, was runner-up in the French Open, and carried off medals innumerable, including all the principal prizes of the R & A.

In all matters sporting, Crawley was a theorist and perfectionist – so much so that it sometimes almost seemed that the method was more important than the result. There was no finer swinger of a club in the world of golf, and on the technique of the game he was an expert to whom came many players of quality, including professionals, for advice generously given. His distinctly fierce, ruddy-complexioned, moustachioed figure was as well-known on courses in the United States as in Britain, and his reports and opinions, often trenchantly expressed, carried much weight during his 25 years as golf correspondent. In particular he was a passionate advocate of the larger ball.

As a cricketer, Leonard came first to light in 1921 by making a hundred for Harrow against Eton at Lord's. He played three times for Cambridge in the University Match and with 98 in 1925 just missed the distinction of his uncle Eustace, who made hundreds in both classic fixtures in the 1880s. As an undergraduate he topped the Worcestershire averages two years running, but at this point his qualification was questioned. He later joined Essex.

In 1925–26 he went with MCC to the West Indies, and if he had been able to play more regularly in 1936, as the selectors hoped, he might well have won a place in G. O. Allen's team to Australia. His most famous innings was the match-winning 176 not out at Leyton for Essex against Sussex, made in three hours and including two hits off Maurice Tate onto the pavilion roof. He was predominantly a forward player, a driver who might have been marvellously suited by Australian pitches.

But there were other strings to his bow. He was a blue for rackets, as well as cricket and golf, won the Northern Lawn Tennis Doubles Championships (with his uncle), as well as a gold medal for ice-skating, and was an outstanding shot. Leonard Crawley in his looks and talk was a survival from Edwardian England. Congratulating a young couple of whose engagement he warmly approved he wrote that it was the best news he had had since Hobbs and Sutcliffe batted all day for England at Melbourne. His friends will recall his idiosyncrasies with humorous affection, while those with whom he crossed swords – and there were some – will remember with respect and regard a formidable adversary.

'DULEEP'

Greatness unfulfilled

Duleepsinhji, Kumar Shri   Amateur

b: Sarodar, India, 13 June 1905

Sch: Cheltenham   *Teams:* Sussex, Cambridge U., Hindus, MCC, England

Career batting:
205-333-23-15485-333-49.95; hundreds 50-*ct* 256
Bowling: 1345-28-48.03

Test batting:
12-19-2-995-173-58.52; hundreds 3-*ct* 10
Bowling 7-0

d: Bombay, India, 5 December 1959. Aged 54.

K. S. Duleepsinhji was a great cricketer, one of the most gifted, as well as most graceful, who ever played for England. Considering that his health allowed him only seven full seasons, his achievements are memorable enough. But news of his death aroused a pang as well as a distant echo, both among those who played with him and those who watched him play, because of the man he was. When the old heroes are talked about and his name is mentioned people will say 'Ah, Duleep!' – and the pause tells of affection as well as respect, for he was a most modest, gentle person. One almost recalls the charm of his character before his merits as a cricketer.

As a batsman he was unquestionably the best amateur between the wars. Indeed, he had no technical superior among the professionals and it is only the extreme brevity of his prime that prevents comparison with Hammond, Hutton and Compton. Most of the great batsmen have been at their best between 25 and 35; 'Duleep' was finished at 27. Only Hammond rivalled him as a slip fieldsman, while in two summers his intelligent, persuasive leadership left an indelible mark on Sussex cricket. The county would not still be looking for its first Championship if he had been spared to play another year or two, perhaps a bare fortnight more.

Duleepsinhji learned his cricket at Cheltenham, and he duly crowned his career as a schoolboy with a hundred for the Lord's Schools. He was lucky in his teachers at school, W. A. Woof, a household word in Gloucestershire in his day, and afterwards in the incomparable Aubrey Faulkner. They for their part had unique natural gifts to work on, plus the magical tradition of his uncle 'Ranji'. If anything was certain it was that 'Duleep' was born to greatness on the cricket field. His career was divided into two phases by the first onset of the tuberculosis which later caused his retirement. After two auspicious years in the Cambridge XI he began 1927 at Fenner's with a hundred against Yorkshire. He followed it with a fabulous 154 not out (wearing two sweaters!) against Middlesex, and was taken that same night into the Addenbrooke Hospital. The end of this prelude to greatness was a year in Switzerland.

Five seasons more, as it turned out, were left to him. During that time he made nearly 10,000 runs for Sussex with an average of 50, scored three hundreds at Lord's against the Players, two of them in the same match, toured New Zealand and Australia with A. H. H. Gilligan's team, and, of course, took his rightful place at number four for England following Hobbs, Sutcliffe, and Hammond. The 173 against Australia in the classic Lord's Test of 1930 was the peak of his achievement. Holding the innings together, he yet scored his runs in four hours and three-quarters. An element of tactical indecision may have helped his end. When he was caught at long-off off Grimmett at quarter-past six, and his uncle the Jam Saheb was remarking 'the boy was always careless', A. C. MacLaren, an oracle of awesome reasonance, was deploring Percy Chapman's criminal folly in not having declared already. The truth was no one then knew quite how to wage a four-day Test. Bradman was soon to show them. In this innings against Grimmett at his best, and in many others against the foremost bowlers of his day, Larwood and Voce, McDonald, Tate, J. C. White, Freeman and the rest, 'Duleep' showed himself the complete artist. He had all the strokes, but as with an earlier aristocrat, William Beldam, his special glory was the cut.

He was as lissom and keen of eye as was to be expected from his race. But he did not presume upon his gifts to flaunt the book.

He, if anyone, put a bloom on the orthodox. And what a bloom! One day he was cutting McDonald to smithereens at Old Trafford, the next, silk shirt a-flutter, he was dancing out to Freeman at Hastings and reducing that tormentor of the slow-footed to utter impotence. Freeman! I only heard once of 'Duleep' getting angry, and Tich Freeman was the sufferer. In dry weather Sussex got caught on a most suspiciously wet wicket at Maidstone and were promptly spun to destruction. 'Duleep' said ominously: 'Wait till they come to Hastings.'

Kent came and he murdered them to the tune of 115 in the first innings and 246 in the second. In these innings he scored at more than 70 an hour off his own bat, and gave in all two hard chances. Once, against Northampton, on the first day of the season at Hove he made 333, and was out by six o'clock. No wonder he swiftly became, and still is, a legend in Sussex. In mid-August 1932, Sussex and Yorkshire were fighting out the Championship toe to toe. At Taunton against Somerset, 'Duleep's' 90 won the match. It was his last innings. His illness had returned, Sussex lost their leader, and MCC had to find a replacement to send with D. R. Jardine's team to Australia. But that rancorous tour, in retrospect anyway, 'Duleep' would have been thankful to miss. Cricket to him was not that sort of game.

BILLY GRIFFITH

MCC's devoted servant

Griffith, Stewart Cathie, CBE, DFC　　　　　　Amateur

b: Wandsworth, London, 16 June 1914

Sch: Dulwich　　　*Teams:* Cambridge U., Surrey, Sussex, MCC, England

Career batting:
215-336-41-4846-140-16.42; hundreds 3-*ct* 328-*st* 80
Bowling: 23-0

Test batting:
3-5-0-157-140-31.40; hundreds 1-*ct* 5

d: Middleton, Sussex,　7 April 1993. Aged 78.

On the matting pitch at Port of Spain Billy Griffith accomplished one of the more celebrated and romantic feats of cricket history. The MCC party was so plagued with injury that Gubby Allen sent him in first. The result was that at the end of a first day of extreme heat and humidity the reserve wicket-keeper and tail-end batsman emerged drained but undefeated with 110. It was the only known instance of a man's sweat coming through to the front of his pads. In his first Test match he had made his maiden first-class hundred. Next day he went on to 140, the match being drawn. A year later in South Africa, he confirmed for permanent record his stature as a wicket-keeper when he was preferred for two Tests to Godfrey Evans. As a stumper his technique was quiet, unshowy. His cricket philosophy was perfectly captured by R. C. Robertson-Glasgow: 'He keeps open house behind the stumps; gives you the sense that conversation is being resumed rather than begun . . . then he accepts your mistake with the ease of the perfect host, and you take the old high-road to the pavilion.'

Three years of cricket writing gave little opportunity to play, and in 1952 he began 22 years of service at Lord's. The next decade saw a singularly happy partnership as one of two assistant secretaries (J. G. Dunbar being the other) to Ronny Aird, whose reign as Secretary, after a long apprenticeship as assistant, epitomised the old, easy, courteous aura traditional to Lord's and MCC. Billy would have made an ideal touring manager, but as each opportunity occurred in this period the excuse was made that he could not be spared. The nearest he got was to substitute for a month in Australia over the 1962–63 New Year, when the manager, the late Duke of Norfolk, had to fly home temporarily on state business.

When in 1962 Griffith succeeded to the Secretaryship there were both change and conflict in the offing, and it was his nature to grieve long and deeply over several of the happenings of his 12 years in office. The economic crisis that hit cricket in the 1960s coincided with the arrival of the Sports Council, set up and funded by Government with power to give financial help to the ruling bodies of sport. This period also saw the beginning of commercial sponsorship. Both these things pointed to a change in the loose governance of the game by MCC, and the responsibility for shaping a generally acceptable new structure devolved upon Gubby Allen as Treasurer of the club and Griffith as Secretary. Hence the establishment in 1968 of the Cricket Council, of the Test and County Cricket Board and the National Cricket Association. Until his retirement Griffith was Secretary of both Council and Board as well as of MCC. Naturally the new pattern had its difficulties, as had the earlier abolition of the amateur , the open-door policy towards overseas cricketers, and the swift acceptance of the limited-overs game as a panacea for the anxieties of the counties.

The event that went deepest to the heart of this most sensitive man, however, was 'the D'Oliveira Affair', the consequent rupture of relations with South Africa, and the criticism, from within as well as without, of MCC for its conduct in the matter. This caused Griffith to offer his resignation, which the Committee unhesitatingly declined. He was appointed CBE in 1975.

It was characteristic of him that at the request of the International Cricket Conference he should have undertaken immediately on his retirement chief responsibility for a complete revision of the Laws. Hence the new, clearer and simplified Code of 1980, only the fifth such since MCC undertook the first at the club's formation in 1787. This daunting exercise might be thought his most enduring memorial. There is, however, another, possibly even more permanent. At the request of Lavinia, Duchess of Norfolk, soon after Duke Bernard's death in 1975, Billy set to work to ensure the continuance of cricket at Arundel. He formed the new Friends of Arundel Park CC and so (with the compliance of the present Duke) ensured a safe future for the game in one of its most idyllic settings.

Few of his predecessors had done more to deserve the presidency of MCC, to which he was appointed in 1979. The celebration of the Centenary Test Match came on top of the heavy duties nowadays demanded of the president, and his health was barely equal to the strain. He ended his year of office in 1980 exhausted, and within a month was enduring a major operation. From this, partial recovery allowed him only an inactive retirement. His closing years were spent in a nursing home, where he was visited daily by his wife. In a last public appearance he emerged briefly for the opening by the Prince of Wales of the cricket school on the Arundel ground which caters chiefly for state schoolchildren.

HAROLD LARWOOD

In his prime the fastest

Larwood, Harold, MBE   Professional

b: Nuncargate, Nottinghamshire, 14 November 1904

Sch: Kirkby Woodhouse Board School   *Teams:* Nottinghamshire,
                                                Europeans, MCC, England

Career batting:
361-438-72-7289-102*-19.91; hundreds 3-*ct* 234
Bowling: 24994-1427-17.51-98-20-9/41

Test batting:
21-28-3-485-98-19.40; *ct* 15
Bowling: 2212-78-28.35

d: Sydney, Australia, 22 July 1995. Aged 90.

Harold Larwood was the most feared and celebrated fast bowler of his time. 'Lol' Larwood had long been the sole survivor of the first Tests in which he played, the memorable series of 1926 when England won back the Ashes. Among modern England cricketers only R. E. S. Wyatt, who died in April 1995 aged 93, approached him in playing seniority: Wyatt's first Tests were in South Africa in 1927–28.

Larwood's international career would certainly have been longer but for the MCC tour to Australia of 1932–33, in which he and his captain D. R. Jardine were the central figures in the most bitter and protracted confrontation that has ever darkened the game. Jardine was the tactical brain, and Larwood and his county colleague, the left-arm Bill Voce, were the chief executors of a new type of bowling labelled 'bodyline'. This was an apt description because both bowlers aimed to pitch the ball short, in the neighbourhood of the batsman's ribs, in order to induce a catch to one of the five or even six close fielders on the leg-side as the batsman aimed to escape being hit on the body.

The method adopted by Jardine owed something to prior discussion with the Notts captain A. W. Carr, who at times in previous seasons had encouraged his two fast bowlers to fire away short at the body to a strong legside field. On the faster Australian pitches Larwood's extreme accuracy had immediate effect, and soon aroused Australian protest. By the third Test at Adelaide, Australian resentment and the reactions of the crowd had reached such a pitch that the Australian Board sent the first of a lengthy exchange of cables to MCC: 'Bodyline bowling has assumed such proportions as to menace the best interests of the game. This is causing intensely bitter feeling between the players, as well as injury. In our opinion, it is unsportsmanlike.' At the insistence of MCC, the board subsequently withdrew the charge of 'unsportsmanlike' behaviour. After two batsmen, Bill Woodfull and Bertie Oldfield, had been painfully struck, mounted troops were assembled behind the pavilion lest Bradman, the popular hero, should be laid low and spectators rush the field in revenge.

The new tactics had been devised in an effort to prevent Bradman's batting from monopolising an England–Australia rubber, as it had done in England two years earlier. By speed of footwork and swift reaction Bradman avoided being hit and emerged from the series at the head of the averages with 56; such was his reputation that this figure was rated a failure. The cost, though, was a row that shook Anglo–Australian relations to the roots, and took all the savour out of victory. When, belatedly, the true nature of the English attack was appreciated at Lord's, MCC made such a method illegal. Though short fast bowling with intimidatory intent is a perennial issue, there have been no subsequent attempts at a repetition of the 1932–33 tactics, with the crescent of close leg-side fielders. In the Bodyline series Larwood took 33 wickets at 19 runs apiece, and so had the major share in bringing home the Ashes. But it was an expensive success for Larwood as well as for English cricket, because in the fifth Test the constant pounding of his left foot on the hard pitches resulted in a fracture in the big toe which ended his career as a truly fast bowler.

The next summer he could play for Notts only as a batsman; he had five more English seasons before retiring at the age of 33, bowling usually at a sharp medium pace with an occasional fast ball. Whether or not in this guise Larwood would have again been chosen for England (as Voce was), the possibility was discounted by certain inflammatory writing ghosted under his name in the popular press, which put him out of court with the authorities. He

36

was, in short, manipulated in a way much more common nowadays than it was then.

A cricketer of the old breed from the coalfields of Nottinghamshire and Derbyshire, Harold Larwood left the pits for Trent Bridge in 1924, and two years later a slim but finely proportioned young man of medium height made his first appearances for England. For the next seven years he was, without argument, the fastest bowler in world cricket. Indeed, those who saw him at the closest quarters during the tour of 1932–33 maintained that his speed had never been equalled. Such estimates, of course, are impossible to prove, but it cannot be doubted that the general intimidatory effect was unparalleled. As far as personal relations were concerned, the end of the story redeems much. When in 1949 MCC decided to offer honorary membership to celebrated old professionals Larwood's name was on the first list. A year later at the instigation of J. H. Fingleton and John Arlott, he moved with his family to Sydney, where he was warmly welcomed.

In later years English visitors found him alert and lively of mind, though his eyesight deteriorated and in the end he was almost blind. Larwood married in 1928, and had five daughters.

MAURICE LEYLAND
'Ah've got him skinned'

Leyland, Maurice   Professional

b: New Park, Harrogate, Yorkshire, 20 July 1900

Teams: Yorkshire, Patiala, MCC, England

Career batting:
686-932-101-33660-263-40.50; hundreds 80-*ct* 246
Bowling: 13659-466-29.31

Test batting:
41-65-5-2764-187-46.06; hundreds 9-*ct* 13
Bowling: 585-6-97.50

d: Scotton Banks, Harrogate, Yorkshire, 1 January 1967. Aged 66.

Maurice Leyland died after several years of sickness most stoically borne. There are certain games-players whose qualities of character are such that they are, from early days, marked out by the crowd and hailed as friends. Such a one was Leyland, of Yorkshire and England, a great batsman of the between-wars period, and a great sportsman, whose stocky figure, with cap slightly a-tilt, was hailed with warmth and respect wherever cricket is played.

Leyland won his county cap in 1922, and so was brought up in the strongest of all Yorkshire schools with Rhodes and Kilner, Robinson and Macaulay, Sutcliffe, Holmes and Oldroyd. From early days his left-handed batsmanship was shaped in a more fluid mould than that of most of his northern contemporaries. His play was effective rather than graceful, and quickness of eye and foot made up for the fact that the bat sometimes strayed a longish way from the perpendicular. Yet he was a magnificent cover-point driver. He cut well too, and altogether made more runs than most of his kind on the off-side. As a young man he was a remarkably fast outfielder, and with a side less well-served could have become a useful slow left-arm bowler of the orthodox kind. As it was, he amused himself when occasionally called upon by bowling 'chinamen' (left-arm off-breaks) – a phrase he is generally credited with inventing.

The first of his six MCC tours was to India in 1926–7. Two years later, amid something of a furore, he was chosen for Australia in preference to Woolley, who, in 1928, scored 3,352 runs, an aggregate then exceeded in an English summer only by Tom Hayward. England's batting was so strong that Leyland did not play in a Test match until the fifth at Melbourne, where he distinguished himself by making 137 and 53 not out on his first appearance against Australia. This was the first of his 41 matches for England. His figures bear out the accepted idea that he was a better Test than county batsman. In 1932, by the time August came he had made only about 700 runs. Just in time he collected 1,000 inside a month, went out to Australia after all, and played his full part in the Test series. A third time he went to Australia, four years later, and with Hammond supported a weak batting side so admirably that England went astonishingly near repeating the victories of the previous two tours. It was on this tour that his moral ascendancy over O'Reilly, at that time the greatest bowler in the world, was fully established and acknowledged. Maurice was a modest man (like most of the very best performers of his generation), but he was not above exploiting a bit of gamesmanship in the cause. 'Ah've got him skinned,' he was reported as saying. A pause, and then: 'and he knows it!'

Besides his three tours to Australia, one of which also involved New Zealand, and then one to India he went also with MCC to South Africa and West Indies. His biggest Test score was his last: 187 at The Oval in 'Hutton's Match' in '38. It was scarcely a characteristic innings, for it was scored on a wicket of pluperfect ease against somewhat ordinary bowling – apart from that of his old antagonist, O'Reilly. His best self was seen when the going was tough. Indeed no more courageous or determined cricketer ever buckled on pads for England.

PHILIP MEAD

A Hampshire institution

Mead, Charles Philip   Professional

b: Battersea, London, 9 March 1887

Sch: Shillingstone Street School, Battersea   *Teams:* Hampshire,
MCC, England,
Tennyson to Jamaica

Career batting:
814-1340-185-55061-280*-47.67; hundreds 153-*ct* 671
Bowling: 9613-277-34.70

Test batting:
17-26-2-1185-182*-49.37; hundreds 4-*ct* 4

d: Boscombe, Hampshire, 26 March 1958. Aged 71.

Few men in the history of English cricket have held the middle of the stage so long as Philip Mead. Only three men, Sir Jack Hobbs, F. E. Woolley, and E. Hendren have scored more runs, and none of these meant more to their respective counties than Mead to Hampshire. Between 1905 and 1936 he made 55,061 runs, with an average of 47. Almost from the moment of his making a century against Yorkshire in his first county match, he bore the brunt of the Hampshire batting. He made a hundred against every county in the Championship. His total bag was 161 hundreds, and in his 50th and last year of first-class cricket he was still the leading Hampshire batsman.

Though his long and devoted service to Hampshire was his chief title to fame, he went twice each to Australia and South Africa with MCC and he played at least one great Test innings at home – his 182 not out against Gregory and McDonald and Warwick Armstrong's Australians in 1921. Mead was born at Battersea, and his career started as a lad on the Surrey ground staff. But he soon gravitated south and according to legend trudged his way from The Oval to Southampton. There he established himself within a few years as the senior professional of a famous quartet which, from humble beginnings, brought great glory to Hampshire: Mead, Kennedy, Newman and Brown. Mead was a large, broad, solid left-hander with limitless patience and remarkable powers of defence. His bland countenance radiated utter calm. There was an air of inevitability about his possession of the crease which made him just about as depressing a man to bowl to as anyone between the eras of Scotton and Woodfull.

Even the complicated ritual with which he prepared for each ball had an inexorable rhythm. First, holding the bat upright with his left hand he gave several little tugs to the cap with the other. When he then assembled his stance he tapped the bat two or three times in the block-hole. Finally, having at first stood so far to leg-ward that the bowler, running up, got an encouraging view of the stumps, he gradually shuffled up to the bat, closing the gap tight shut. Neither his stance nor his style were classically fashioned, but to the cricketer no one who met the ball so consistently with the middle of such a seemingly wide bat could be described as an ugly player. And though never setting out to dominate an attack, he was usually pushing his score along much less slowly than it seemed.

He was a fine, meaty cutter, and put his weight solidly into the left-hander's cover drive. There was little impression of effort, but, as with all masters, exact timing gave pace. In an age when there was far less bowling on the leg-side of the wicket, he was the safest of collectors off his pads. He loved fast bowling, and particularly enjoyed making runs on turning wickets. The most dangerous spinners would as soon have bowled to Hobbs or Hammond when the ball was talking.

It happened that the first Test I ever saw was the scene of his most famous innings. He was not sent to Australia with Douglas's team just after the First World War, and England had lost eight Tests running against Armstrong's team in little more than six months. When the captaincy was handed over to Lionel Tennyson, he immediately secured Mead's selection, and also that of Brown. These three men of Hampshire had most to do with breaking the malign spell. One retains a clear boyhood impression of Gregory and McDonald wearing bare tracks up to the Oval wickets, and of Mead batting on and on as impervious to their speed as to the sharp wrist-spin of Arthur Mailey. And, be it noted, the slowcoach's 182 was made in just five hours.

Mead came of a generation of professionals which had to be satisfied with modest rewards. His two benefits for 32 years of service brought him just £1,642. Soon after he retired he lost the sight of one eye, and latterly was completely blind. Like Wilfred Rhodes, he bore his affliction with stoic cheerfulness, and it was one of the pleasanter experiences to see him on the Bournemouth ground, surrounded by the young Hampshire team, modestly reminiscing, watching the game in progress, as it were, from memory.

ERNEST TYLDESLEY

'Very interested in cricket'

Tyldesley, George Ernest

b: Roe Green, Worsley, Lancashire, 5 February 1889

Sch: Salford School of Technology   *Teams:* Lancashire, MCC,
England, Joel to South
Africa, Tennyson
to Jamaica

Career batting:
648-961-106-38874-256*-45.46; hundreds 102-*ct* 293
Bowling: 346-6-57.66

Test batting:
14-20-2-990-122-55.00; hundreds 3-*ct* 2
Bowling: 2-0

d: Rhos-on-Sea, Denbighshire, 5 May 1962. Aged 73.

Ernest Tyldesley's death at the age of 73 shortened the select list of great cricketers who made the beginnings of their fame before the First War. No one who watched or played with him would question his title to greatness, while figures confirm it handsomely. He reached 1,000 runs 19 times, and in 1928, that rich batting year, got 3,024. He went with MCC both to Australia and South Africa, and was never seen to better advantage than on the matting wickets in the Union. He was coming up to his prime when the First War came: hence he was chosen for only 14 Tests, in which he averaged 55. If for all his accomplishments Tyldesley was not often an automatic choice for England it must be remembered also that he lived in prosperous times.

For instance, he had a wonderful run of success in the midsummer of 1926, making 1,128 runs in nine successive innings with an average of 141. He was duly chosen for the fourth Test at

Old Trafford, made 81, yet could not find a place in the Oval Test when the Ashes were won. England's chief batsmen then were Hobbs, Sutcliffe, Woolley and Hendren, with the imperious figure of Hammond soon standing in his way.

Tyldesley had about him an unruffled serenity which was reflected in his play. He was a well-nigh perfect technician with a particular facility off his legs and as a cutter. For Lancashire he was normally a model of consistency at No. 3. Over his career he averaged 45. With F. Watson he once, against Surrey, made 371 for the second wicket.

He was one of the first professionals to be elected to a county committee, and in that capacity did long and valuable service at Old Trafford until his health began to fail, and, like two of his famous contemporaries Philip Mead and Wilfred Rhodes, he practically lost his sight. I remember Ernest once being buttonholed after the day's cricket at Old Trafford by one of the game's most pertinacious talkers, to whom he gave his usual quiet and courteous attention. All sorts of high technicalities were propounded by the chatty one, who was heard afterwards to say, 'That old fellow seems very interested in cricket. What's his name?' He was told, 'You were talking to Ernest Tyldesley.' It is a little story somehow so characteristic of this most charming and self-effacing man.

BRYAN VALENTINE

Kentish to the core

Valentine, Bryan Herbert, MC   Amateur

b: Blackheath, Kent, 17 January 1908

Sch: Repton   *Teams:* Kent, Cambridge U., MCC, England,
                     Tennyson to Jamaica

Career batting:
399-645-38-18306-242-30.15; hundreds 35-*ct* 289
Bowling: 1125-27-41.66

Test batting:
7-9-2-454-136-64.85; hundreds 2-*ct* 2

d: Otford, Kent, 2 February 1983. Aged 75.

Bryan Valentine was a splendid cricketer for Cambridge, Kent
and England and, almost from his emergence as a Repton
schoolboy, a universally popular figure. Though cricket was the
love of his life, he was an all-round sportsman who won the
Public Schools lawn tennis doubles for Repton partnering the subsequently famous Bunny Austin, as well as gaining his blue at soccer and cricket. He also became a scratch golfer.

He played first for Kent as a schoolboy and, although with his
free wristy style he needed a year or two to tighten his defence in
county cricket, by 1932 he was one of the leading amateur batsmen. Chosen for D. R. Jardine's MCC tour of India in 1933–34, he
made 136 at Bombay in his first Test. Under A. P. F. Chapman,
with Ashdown, Woolley, Ames and Valentine at the top of the
order, with the captain and other strokemakers to follow, Kent had
as attractive a batting side as any in the country. On Chapman's
retirement he shared the leadership for one summer with R. T., the
middle of the three Bryan brothers, and in 1938–39 went with
W. R. Hammond's MCC side to South Africa. There he made

another Test hundred at Cape Town. With the onset of war he had no further chance for England, so ending with a batting average for his seven Tests of 64.

Badly wounded during the war, when he won the MC, he was still able to take on the captaincy of Kent from 1946 to 1948 and even had his supporters to lead England abroad. He would have done it well for he was always cheerful and everyone enjoyed playing under him. If it could be said of any man that he never had an enemy it could be said of Bryan.

Nine times he made 1,000 in a season. He was president of Kent CCC in 1967.

BILL VOCE
Left-arm – and fast

Voce, William   Professional

b: Annesley Woodhouse, Nottinghamshire, 8 August 1909

Teams: Nottinghamshire, MCC, England

Career batting:
426-525-130-7590-129-19.21; hundreds 4-*ct* 286
Bowling: 35961-1558-23.08

Test batting:
27-38-15-308-66-13.39; *ct* 15
Bowling: 2733-98-27.88

d: Nottingham, 6 June 1984. Aged 74.

The name of Bill Voce, one of the best of all left-arm fast bowlers, will be associated for ever in history with that of his great partner for Notts and England, Harold Larwood. Together they had the chief part in winning the County Championship of 1929: together, under the stern instruction of the captain, D. R. Jardine, they perfected in the 1932–33 Test series in Australia the fast leg-theory attack which came to be known as bodyline. Larwood so injured his left foot on that tour that he could never again recapture anything approaching his phenomenal speed, though he soldiered on for several more seasons of county cricket at fast-medium pace in company with Voce, his junior by five years.

Both before and after the Bodyline tour the Notts bowling, on the orders of the captain, A. W. Carr, sometimes over-stepped the margin of fair play, and it was not until Notts put the leadership into more acceptable hands that relations with several of the counties were repaired.

Happily, too, though Larwood's Test days were past, the breach with Lord's that had prevented Voce's selection for England for four of his prime seasons was healed, and he sailed for Australia again with G. O. Allen's team for the 1936–37 tour.

With 26 wickets at 21 runs each he headed England's Test bowling averages, and such was the paucity of talent after the Second World War that in his 38th year he made a third tour to Australia in 1946–47. The spirit still was as willing as ever but of the fire and elasticity of that bounding run and classical delivery only spasmodic vestiges remained. Circumstances, then, prevented Voce from building up over a long but interrupted career figures which would have better reflected his skills.

Voce as a tall, slim lad walked from the colliery town of Hucknall to Trent Bridge in the late twenties in search of a trial. There his natural talent was at once recognised. He had a long, loose arm and a natural flowing action, with the ability, bowling over the wicket, to swing the ball either way in the air. After the shine had gone, now round the wicket, he straightened the ball still at lively speed, unless the conditions suggested slow-medium spin. He was indeed an artist and an athlete quite out of the ordinary.

Bill, after his retirement, was in much demand as a coach, and at the age of 70 was still wheeling away at Lord's at the MCC Indoor School and enthusing the boys with his humour and friendliness.

ARTHUR WELLARD
Five hundred sixes!

Wellard, Arthur William   Professional

b: Southfleet, Kent, 8 April 1902

Teams: Somerset, MCC, England, Tennyson to India

Career batting:
417-679-46-12485-112-19.72; hundreds 2-*ct* 376
Bowling: 39302-1614-24.35

Test batting:
2-4-0-47-38-11.75; *ct* 2
Bowling: 237-7-33.85

d: Eastbourne, Sussex, 31 December 1980. Aged 78.

Arthur Wellard, of Somerset, was a cricketer after every school-boy's heart, an ever-cheerful all-rounder and, above all, a prodigious hitter of sixes. In a career of 15 playing seasons, on either side of the war, he hit 500 of them, a much larger number than anyone before or since, though it must be remembered that in G. L. Jessop's day only hits out of the ground counted six. Twice on the Wells ground, admittedly a small one, Wellard struck five sixes in an over, a sequence unequalled until Gary Sobers smote all six balls beyond the Swansea boundary many years later. Wellard, however, was no mere slogger. With enormous hands and using a bat little short of 3lb weight, he had a sound defence and is one of the few all-rounders to have made as many as 12,485 runs and (as a fast-medium bowler who could also turn to off-spinners) taken 1,614 wickets.

He played in only two Tests, and against Australia at Lord's in 1938, in a thrilling stand of 74 with young Denis Compton, helped save England from defeat, depositing a ball from McCabe in the

Grandstand balcony in the process. He was chosen to go with MCC to India in 1940, and a better tourist it would be hard to imagine.

Wellard was born in Kent, but was reputedly told when applying for a job on the ground-staff that he had much better become a policeman, a story, wrote R. L. Arrowsmith in *Barclays World of Cricket*, which 'will seem improbable only to those who have never tried to judge young cricketers'. He qualified for Somerset where he fitted the scene perfectly, a spiritual descendant if ever there was one of that immortal West Country hero, Sammy Woods.

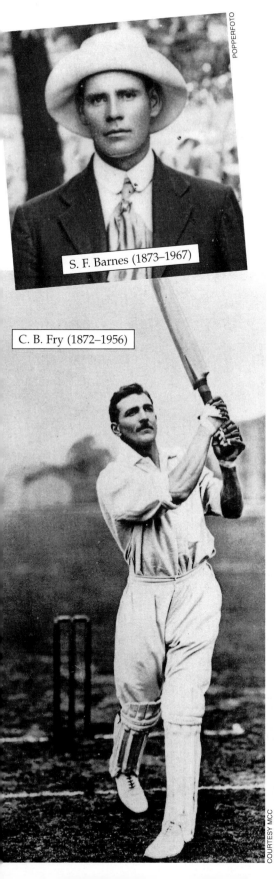

S. F. Barnes (1873–1967)

C. B. Fry (1872–1956)

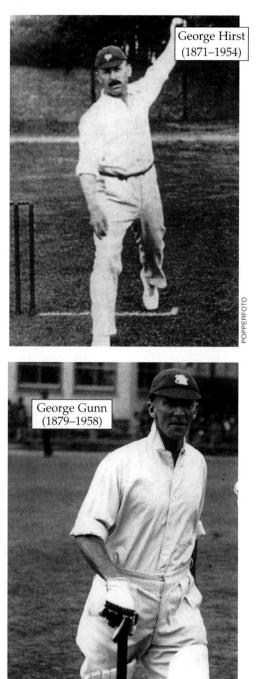

George Hirst
(1871–1954)

George Gunn
(1879–1958)

Reggie Spooner (1880–1961)

Wilfred Rhodes (1877–1973)

Sir Pelham Warner (1873–1963)

Bill Bowes
(1908–1987)

Frank Chester
(1895–1957)

Leonard Crawley (1903–1981)

Maurice Leyland (1900–1967)

K. S. Duleepsinhji (1905–1959)

Harold Larwood (1904–1995)

'Billy' Griffith (1914–1993)

Ernest Tyldesley
(1889–1962)

Philip Mead (1887–1958)

Arthur Wellard (1902–1980)

Bryan Valentine (1908–1983)

Bill Voce (1909–1984)

Gerry Chalk (1910–1943)

Peter Eckersley (1904–1940)

Kenneth Farnes (1911–1941)

G. B. Legge (1903–1940)

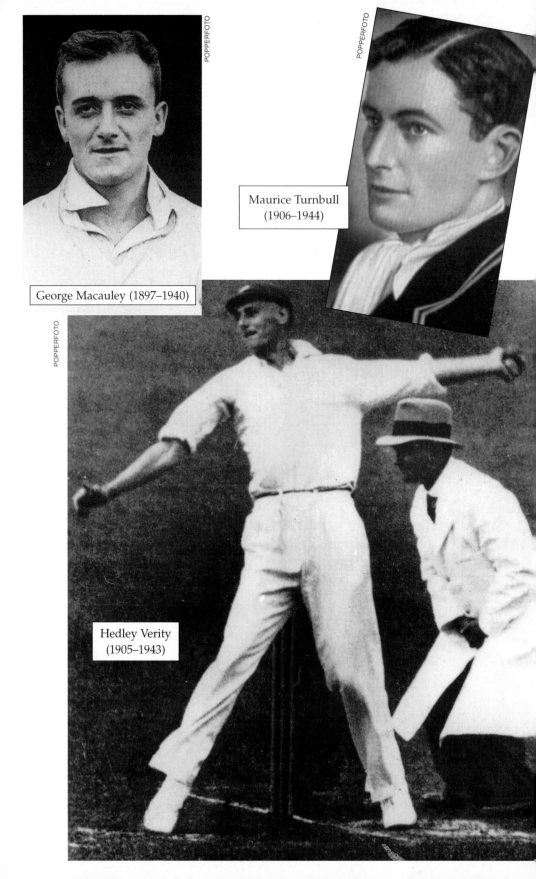

Maurice Turnbull
(1906–1944)

George Macauley (1897–1940)

Hedley Verity
(1905–1943)

3
ROLL OF HONOUR

GERRY CHALK

A born captain

Chalk, Frederick Gerald Hudson, DFC   Amateur

b: Sydenham, 7 September 1910

Sch: Uppingham   *Teams:* Kent, Oxford U.

Career batting:
156-259-20-6732-198-28.16; hundreds 11-*ct* 62
Bowling: 409-7-58.42

d: Louches, nr. Calais, 17 February 1943. Aged 32.

There were few more glamorous figures in county cricket when war brought the season of 1939 to a halt than the young captain of Kent who became one of its more spectacular casualties. Frederick Gerald Hudson Chalk was one of a string of fine cricketers who enjoyed the coaching of Frank Gilligan at Uppingham. At Oxford he played four years for the University, being captain in his last, to which he contributed what *Wisden* described as a 'brilliant' hundred against Cambridge.

After several years as a schoolmaster Chalk captained Kent with an adventurous panache in 1938 and 1939. He led a conspicuously happy side to fifth place in 1939, making a fast 94 against Lancashire at Dover in his last innings. He and Arthur Fagg made an opening stand of 181, and Kent scored 382 for five to win a rousing match. In the previous match, albeit Kent were defeated by Yorkshire, he carried his bat through the second innings for 115 not out.

In the pre-war years no one in county cricket better typified the virtues of amateur – and thus independent – leadership. He never minded suffering defeat in pursuing the prospect of victory, as is testified by the extraordinary fact that of 27 Championship matches Kent drew only 3, one of those ruined by the weather. They had no more effective attacking bowler than Doug Wright, and when it came to chasing a target they had the ideal man in the leading batsman, Leslie Ames, with Bryan Valentine and the captain himself in support. The more solid element was supplied by Fagg and the all-rounder, Leslie Todd.

On the outbreak of war Chalk joined the Honourable Artillery Company as a gunner, but soon transferred to the RAF, and in June 1941 won the DFC as a rear-gunner. The citation recorded that 'Chalk by his cool and accurate fire saved his aircraft and probably destroyed the attacker'. Having survived 30 sorties as a rear-gunner Chalk took a pilot's course and became a Spitfire flight commander. He failed to return from a battle over Boulogne and it was assumed he had come down in the sea until the remains of pilot and aircraft were discovered buried 46 years later in northern France, the body being ascertained by his identity disc. Leslie Ames, Godfrey Evans (who had kept wicket a few times for the county in 1939 as a 17-year-old) and other Kentish personalities joined his widow Rosemary (née Foster) at the funeral, in a military cemetery near Boulogne.

PETER ECKERSLEY

A natural leader

Eckersley, Peter Thorp, MP   Amateur

b: Lowton, Newton-le-Willows, 2 July 1904

Sch: Rugby   *Teams:* Lancashire, MCC, Cahn to Argentina

Career batting:
292-339-51-5629-102*-19.54; hundreds 1-ct 141
Bowling: 348-7-49.71-0-0-2/21

d: Eastleigh, Hampshire, 13 August 1940. Aged 36.

In Peter Eckersley's six summers as captain of Lancashire (1929–35) they won two titles and were once runners-up. They were never lower than sixth. Certainly he inherited from his predecessor, Leonard Green, a side which had been champions three years running. However, Ted McDonald, the great Australian fast bowler, coming up to 40, not surprisingly was losing his menace while Richard Tyldesley, his foil as a spinner, had a disagreement with the club over his salary and suddenly departed for the league. Harry Makepeace, their old faithful, at 47 was on his last legs.

It was no easy inheritance for a young man of 24. From the start, however, Eckersley showed he had the character to hold the side together. The historian of Lancashire, A. W. Ledbrooke, wrote of him that 'he had a natural gift for leadership expressed not by giving orders or making rules but by example and genial personality, and he possessed the rare gift of attracting affectionate friendship'. In the Rugby XI in his last year, he never threatened to win a blue at Cambridge. Yet in additon to brilliant close fielding he was far from being a negligible batsman when the going was tough. When the Australians came to Liverpool in 1930 Eckersley made top score in both innings: and he was one of the heroes – Lionel Lister, his successor, and Ernest Tyldesley, above all, were others – in a gallant victory after an unpleasant, bruising match at Trent Bridge which resulted in Lancashire cancelling fixtures with Notts the following year.

Eckersley had a great love of flying, and often arrived at a match in his own plane. Faced with an awkward journey from Cardiff to Southampton, he chartered two aircraft for the side and in a flight of 50 minutes Lancashire made history. He also had political ambitions, and in the General Election of 1935 became the Unionist member for the Exchange division of Manchester. When war threatened he joined the Air Arm of the RNVR. He had no thought of claiming exemption as a Member of Parliament and a year later was killed in a flying accident.

KENNETH FARNES

A giant on his day

Farnes, Kenneth   Amateur

b: Leytonstone, 8 July 1911

Sch: Liberty GS, Romford   *Teams:* Essex, Cambridge U., MCC,
England

Career batting:
168-201-59-1182-97*-8.32; *ct* 84
Bowling: 14804-690-21.45

Test batting:
15-17-5-58-20-4.83; *ct* 1
Bowling: 1719-60-28.65

d: Chipping Warden, Oxfordshire, 20 October 1941. Aged 30.

Ken was a giant of 6ft 5in with a physique to match, who on his day, from 1933 to the outbreak of war, was the fastest and most formidable opening bowler in England. The qualification is made because it seemed that something extra might be needed to rouse him to full steam. It could be a fresh Essex seaside pitch, or the sight of Yorkshire, the champions of the last pre-war years. In 1934 he took 11 wickets against them to bring about an innings defeat, Essex's first victory against Yorkshire since 1911. At least once he wanted to prevent the selectors overlooking his claims. In 1938 he played against Australia with fair success in the first two Tests but was dropped for the third, which in fact was abandoned without a ball bowled. The Gentlemen and Players match then took place before the next Test side was due to be picked. After the amateurs had made 411 the professionals were subjected to some of the fastest bowling, so said the seasoned critics, that was ever seen at Lord's. His analysis was eight for 43. In the second innings came more, and a victory for the Gents by 133 runs. The point was taken, and Farnes played not only in the last two Tests but was chosen to tour South Africa that winter.

Farnes had a model action, needing only eleven paces to bring the arm high over with the maximum effect. He was discovered playing for Gidea Park when Percy Perrin, the old Essex batsman (and future Test selector), took the Club and Ground side there in 1930. He at once made his mark for Essex, who were always glad to have him but could never claim his exclusive services because three years at Cambridge were followed by a teaching post at Worksop. In the University Match of 1933 he was encouraged by Denis Wilcox, his captain, to bowl short to a leg-side field, the bodyline tactic which had caused so much mayhem in Australia a few months earlier. This met with some success, though Oxford struggled to a draw. It was not approved, and was indeed foreign to Farnes's genial nature. On the easy South African pitches Farnes was not effective in Johannesburg's altitude (as other sportsmen have been) but showed his stamina at sea level in the ten-day finale at Durban (which had to be drawn in order for the team to catch the boat home). He bowled 68 eight-ball overs for his five wickets and was Verity's chief support throughout the series.

Farnes was something of an artist and a musician. He came to a tragic end, a plane piloted by him crashing during night-fighter training.

G. B. LEGGE

Malvernian batsmanship

Legge, Geoffrey Bevington, Lieut.-Com.   Amateur

b: Bromley, Kent, 26 January 1903

Sch: Malvern   *Teams:* Oxford U., Kent, MCC, England

Career batting:
147-210-11-4955-196-24.89; hundreds 7-*ct* 122
Bowling: 181-8-22.62

Test batting:
5-7-1-299-196-49.83; hundreds 1-*ct* 1
Bowling: 34-0

d: Brampford Speke, Devon, 21 November 1940. Aged 37.

Geoffrey Legge, who was killed while flying in the RNVR Fleet Air Arm, was captain in turn of Malvern, Oxford and Kent. He toured twice with MCC sides, first with R.T. Staniforth to South Africa and then under A. H. H. Gilligan to New Zealand and Australia. He played in five Tests abroad and in his last at Auckland made a handsome 196 in four and a half hours.

Legge was a typical Malvern batsman in the coaching era of Charles Toppin, full of wristy off-side strokes encouraged by the short cover-point boundaries, very much in the tradition of the Foster brotherhood. He was for three years (1928–30) Kent captain, very much in the free-scoring traditions of the county. In 1928 they were runners-up in the Championship. He was the first of two Kent captains to be killed in the air, Gerry Chalk being the other.

GEORGE MACAULAY
Pillar of Yorkshire

Macaulay, George Gibson, Pilot Officer   Professional

b: Thirsk, Yorkshire, 7 December 1897

Sch: Barnard Castle   *Teams:* Yorkshire, MCC, England

Career batting:
468-460-125-6056-125*-18.07; hundreds 3-*ct* 373
Bowling: 32440-1837-17.65

Test batting:
8-10-4-112-76-18.66; *ct* 5
Bowling: 662-24-27.58

d: Sullom Voe, Shetland Islands, 13 December 1940. Aged 43.

George Macaulay, an integral member of successive Yorkshire sides between 1920 and 1935, did not win his place therein by the normal route. Educated at Barnard Castle School, on leaving he joined the Royal Field Artillery, and at the end of the First World War pursued a career as a bank clerk. He was 23 when he first emerged in the Yorkshire side as a fast bowler. George Hirst and Wilfred Rhodes, however, saw possibilities in him as a medium-paced off-breaker and in June 1921 at Hull in this guise this young man of strong physique took six Derbyshire wickets for 3 runs. This was the beginning of 15 seasons which brought him 1773 wickets for Yorkshire at 17 runs apiece. He could swing the new ball dangerously and was an intrepid close fielder. His form won him a place in the MCC side which F.T. Mann took to South Africa in 1922–23. He got a wicket with his first ball in Test cricket and he made the winning hit when England got home by one wicket. In four Tests he had 15 more wickets, mostly sharing the new ball on the matting pitches.

In 1924 Middlesex and Surrey objected to Yorkshire's attitude at times on the field and Middlesex declined to arrange fixtures for next season. Waddington was required to make apologies, and Macaulay was rated as not the least vocal member of the side. Things improved under a new captain, Major A. W. Lupton, in 1935 and Middlesex were among Yorkshire's opponents after all.

Macaulay reached the peak of his form in 1925, when he took 211 wickets at 15 runs apiece. The following year he had what could have been the moment of his life when chosen for England for the third Test at Headingley. This was the famous occasion when A. W. Carr put Australia in on a soft pitch, then himself dropped Macartney in the slips in the first over, whereupon in a brilliant innings Macartney scored a hundred before lunch, too many of them off Macaulay, the local hope. Macaulay was unlucky in finding a truly great batsman in wonderful form. He had, however, a surprising part to play in saving the match. At a pinch his wicket was seldom an easy one to get and now he and George Geary, coming together at 182 for eight in reply to Australia's 494, put on 108, Macaulay's share being 76.

Though continuing as an integral part of the Yorkshire attack, he was not again chosen for England for seven years. He took 100 wickets ten times and helped Yorkshire to ten Championships. An injury to his spinning finger led to his resignation in favour of an easier life in league cricket. He joined the RAF in World War Two but as a Pilot Officer soon died of pneumonia in the Shetland Islands.

MAURICE TURNBULL

Saviour of Glamorgan

Turnbull, Maurice Joseph Lawson, Major   Amateur

b: Cardiff, 16 March 1906

Sch: Downside   *Teams:* Glamorgan, Cambridge U., Wales, MCC, England

Career batting:
388-626-37-17544-233-29.78; hundreds 29-*ct* 280
Bowling: 355-4-88.75

Test batting: 9-13-2-224-61-20.36; *ct* 1

d: Nr. Montchamp, France, 5 August 1944. Aged 38.

Cricket sustained one of its most serious war casualties in Maurice Joseph Turnbull, captain in turn of Cambridge and Glamorgan, an all-round sportsman of rare versatility who represented Wales at Rugby football and hockey, the former at scrum-half, and played cricket for England. He was also squash champion of South Wales. Major Turnbull was serving with the Welsh Guards when, in carrying out a reconnaissance during the advance in Normandy, he was killed by a sniper.

He was an admirable batsman of aggressive inclination and an intrepid close fielder who, after coming down from Cambridge, devoted himself whole-heartedly to the affairs of Glamorgan at a time when it seemed that a mistake had been made in admitting them to the County Championship. They were either at the foot of the table or close to it – in one year they won one match and lost 20 – and in the year before Turnbull took over the captaincy no fewer than seven men had led the side. As J. C. Clay, their only cricketer of real class, wrote in *Wisden*, Glamorgan looked to be 'a bedraggled flock without a shepherd'. The club were heavily in debt, and Turnbull, who also took on the Secretaryship, travelled all over Wales to arouse interest and financial support.

Turnbull was a youthful prodigy. In his first match for Glamorgan as a Downside boy of 17 on a difficult pitch at Swansea he made 40, the highest score in the match, against Lancashire, who were defeated in 'the surprise of the season'. In his last year at school he averaged 94.

In his twenties he played six times in Tests, three times at home and on MCC tours to New Zealand and South Africa, about which he collaborated amusingly with M. J. C. Allom in *The Book of the Two Maurices* and *The Two Maurices Again*. He had only moderate success, his defence perhaps lacking somewhat against Test bowling. He was made a Test selector at the tender age of 31. He was an intelligent captain in the quiet mould, equable, never rattled, attributes which served him well likewise in the field of battle.

HEDLEY VERITY

All the virtues

Verity, Hedley, Capt.   Professional

b: Headingley, Leeds, 18 May 1905

Sch: Yeadon and Guiseley Secondary   *Teams:* Yorkshire, MCC,
                                                     England

Career batting:
378-416-106-5605-101-18.08; hundreds 1-*ct* 269
Bowling: 29146-1956-14.90

Test batting: 40-44-12-669-66*-20.90-*ct* 30
Bowling: 3510-144-24.37

d: Caserta, Italy, 31 July 1943. Aged 38.

Hedley Verity, the Yorkshire and England slow left-arm bowler, died of wounds in July 1943, having become a prisoner of war in Italy. As a captain in the Green Howards, leading his company in an attack on a German strong point at Catania in Sicily, he was hit in the chest and saved from burning corn by his batman. 'Keep going! Keep going!' Hedley had been encouraging his men, words that expressed part of his philosophy as a bowler. Not a great spinner of the ball, on good pitches he worked away, tireless, determined, and in length immaculate, relying on subtle variations of pace and angle of delivery.

Given a helpful pitch, he added to these virtues the ability to turn the ball as much as he needed. When the ball would lift as well as turn the results were apt to be spectacular in the extreme. I take the figures which follow from Alan Hill's perceptive biography. In his first full season for Yorkshire, 1931, at Headingley just down the road from his birthplace, he took (on his 26th birthday) all ten Warwickshire wickets for 36 runs. A year later on the same ground he took the most inexpensive all ten in the game's history: 10 for 10 against Nottinghamshire. In 1933 he had the highest bag of his career: 17 for 91 against Essex at Leyton. Twelve months later came the performance which assured his fame, 15 for 104 against Australia at Lord's, all but one after a wet weekend on the third day.

Australia, replying to England's 440, had made 192 for two, needing 99 more with eight wickets in hand to avert the follow-on which, if achieved, would have opened up very different possibilities on a fourth day. I well recall the Australians saying later in the tour that it had never occurred to them before play began that day that they were in danger of following on. The truth is that the pitch, while taking spin, was never inordinately difficult. What undid Australia was unfamiliarity with the conditions and the consequent sharp shift of morale as Verity got to work. When Chipperfield and Oldfield were putting on 40 for the seventh wicket it seemed they might reach the immediate target; but Verity's artistry was never threatened, and when No. 11 succumbed they were 17 runs short. In the second innings perhaps only Bradman could have given Australia any hope of rescue but, in trying to hook Verity, he hit the ball mountains high. Ames, keeping wicket, made the catch and as the Don passed him his captain's look indicated a reprimand. Woodfull stayed for two hours, but when he went the rest followed headlong, and at quarter to six Hedley's Match was over, England having beaten Australia at Lord's for the only time in this century.

Hedley's ten years in the Yorkshire side was the period of the greatest success in their history: six times Champions, twice under F. E. Greenwood followed by four titles under the forceful leadership of Brian Sellers. Such a record could only be possible given a high-class attack and Yorkshire had this in the Verity–Bowes partnership. Bowes's contribution was bowling just short of top pace, likewise well up and from the high action of a very tall man. Bowes could usually move the ball both in the air and off the pitch, and though unathletic in appearance he could 'keep going' for long spells. One thinks of spin bowlers' and opening bowlers' partnerships, but it is doubtful whether any side ever had a more consistently successful alliance of speed and spin over a whole decade. Both were blooded under Alan Barber's admirable leadership in 1930, Wilfred Rhodes's last year.

In the nine seasons following, they averaged between them 265 wickets a year in Championship matches, 1304 to Verity, 1074 to Bowes. Moreover in only one year did the cost of their wickets rise to 20. The average cost was around 14. Verity toured four times, twice to Australia, once each to India and South Africa. Douglas Jardine used him defensively on the Bodyline tour to rest his fast bowlers, and so as a rule did Gubby Allen in 1936–37 when he was the only bowler who could keep Bradman reasonably quiet. Jardine and he had a strong rapport and under the former in India Verity established an early economy which he maintained throughout the three Test series. His 23 wickets at 16 runs apiece was the biggest factor in England's success. On the plumb easy pitches in South Africa in the last pre-war tour, Walter Hammond was happy to see him in his Australian mode and he not only headed the Test averages with 19 wickets but did so at a cost of less than 2 runs an over.

As a batsman he was correct and dependable. Yorkshire did not want runs from him as often as England did, even to the extent of his opening the innings. Not many men picked purely as bowlers have averaged 20 with the bat over a span of 40 Tests. It matches well his record of 144 Test wickets at 24 runs apiece.

As the war clouds gathered in 1939 Verity and Yorkshire signed off with a rare flourish. Ending their season with a southern tour, they beat Kent and Hampshire by an innings and Sussex by 9 wickets. Hedley's match figures were respectively nine for 80, seven for 51 and at Hove, after being freely punished by George Cox in the first innings, came the following analysis: 6 overs, 1 maiden, 9 runs, 7 wickets. The pitch was drying after the previous day's thunderstorm, and in an unreal atmosphere, with the Germans already invading Poland, Verity attended to the business in hand. Sussex were bowled out for 33, and his last analysis was the second best of his career. 'I wonder if I shall ever bowl here again,' he said as the members of a great team boarded the coach to make the final, grim journey back home. When the casualties were counted six years later there was no cricketer whose name was greeted with greater respect and affection.

4

THE WEST INDIAN IMPACT

LEARIE CONSTANTINE
Man for all seasons

Constantine, Baron Learie Nicholas, MBE   Professional

b: Petit Valley, Diego Martin, Trinidad, 21 September 1901

Sch: St Ann's School, Trinidad   *Teams:* Trinidad, West Indies

Career batting:
119-197-11-4475-133-24.05; hundreds 5-*ct* 133
Bowling: 8991-439-20.48

Test batting:
18-33-0-635-90-19.24; *ct* 28
Bowling: 1746-58-30.10

d: Brondesbury, London, 1 July 1971. Aged 69.

L ord Constantine built a life of noted public service in several fields on the original base of his fame as a cricketer. Welfare officer, civil servant, barrister, minister in the Trinidad Government, High Commissioner for his native island in London, member of the Race Relations Board, of the Sports Council and of the General Advisory Council of the BBC: such were the distinctions that came to him when his playing days were over.

Finally in 1969 came the life peerage, in regard to which he said, 'I think it must have been for what I have endeavoured to do to make it possible for people of different colour to know each other better and live well together.' Learie Nicholas Constantine took the title of Baron Constantine of Maraval in Trinidad and Tobago and of Nelson in the County Palatine of Lancaster. He announced in June 1971 that he must leave Britain. He had asthma and had been warned by his doctor that another winter in this country would kill him. He was the first coloured life peer.

In his public and other capacities Lord Constantine made his mark, but in the memory of those who saw him play, or merely read of his exploits, his cricket has a place apart. There have been many all-rounders with better records on paper with both bat and ball; but it is hard to think of one who made a more sensational impact, in either department, and above all impossible to imagine his superior as a fielder anywhere. So far as the English public were concerned, he was the first of the great players from the Caribbean islands. Fast bowler, hitter and performer of every sort of lithe, juggling acrobatics in the field, he indeed personified West Indian cricket from the first faltering entry into the Test arena in 1928 until the post-war emergence of the trinity of Worrell, Weekes and Walcott. Born into a sporting family in the cricketing hotbed of Port of Spain – his father, L. S., had come to England on the second West Indian visit of 1906 – he toured here first as a young man of 21 in 1923, making no real mark except in the field.

His second appearance five years later was a different story from the moment when in early June he brought about a single-handed victory over a powerful Middlesex side to which the history of cricket has few parallels. He reached the double of a thousand runs and a hundred wickets on that tour – one of nine overseas cricketers to have ever done so – without however distinguishing himself in the Tests. And the plain fact is that though Constantine achieved several spectacular things in his 18 Tests his record of 635 runs, average 19, and 58 wickets, average 30, is a poor reflection of his talent. Though general impetuosity (and poor West Indian slip-fielding!) cost him dear, in the highest class Learie Constantine was, need it be said, the ideal Saturday afternoon League cricketer, a magnet without compare before or since.

From 1929 onwards until the mid-50s he made his home in Lancashire. In the war he did a Civil Defence job there until called to London by the Ministry of Labour. Small wonder that in his maturity the town of Nelson bestowed upon him its freedom. Like Sir Frank Worrell after him, he furthered his own education while making his living as a cricketer, being finally admitted to the Bar after various diversions at the ripe age of 54.

None could call Lord Constantine a modest man, but gifts of warmth and friendliness as well as a shrewd brain and ready tongue helped to make him one of the personalities of his time. Back now in Trinidad, he became Minister of Works and Transport in the first party government, and on the granting of independence in 1962 he was knighted on taking up the new post of High Commissioner in London. He married in 1927 Norma Agatha Cox of Port of Spain, Trinidad, and had a daughter.

GERRY GOMEZ

All-rounder in every sense

Gomez, Gerald Ethridge   Amateur

b: Belmont, Port of Spain, Trinidad, 10 October 1919

Sch: Queen's Royal, Trinidad   *Teams:* Trinidad, West Indies

Career batting:
126-182-27-6764-216*-43.63; hundreds 14-*ct* 92
Bowling: 5052-200-25.26

Test batting:
29-46-5-1243-101-30.31; hundreds 1-*ct* 18
Bowling: 1590-58-27.41

d: Trinidad, 6 August 1996. Aged 76.

Gerry Gomez was an outstanding cricketer and a household name in his native Trinidad, and throughout the West Indies. He was a genuine all-rounder. His batting style was far from fluent but, with his gritty determination, he made vital middle-order contributions. Over the years he became increasingly useful as a medium-paced bowler, and learned how to swing the ball in both directions. He is remembered for the way in which he nodded his head during his run-up. Gomez was also a superb close catcher, and claimed 18 Test wickets in this way.

His reputation stretched from 1939, when as a 19-year-old he came first to England with R. S. Grant's team, up to 1996. As president, he was at the centre of a year-long centenary celebration of Queen's Park cricket club. Gomez was a versatile games player who represented Trinidad at football and was also a keen golfer and tennis player. He was proprietor of the sports goods firm of Sports and Games, sometimes known as Sports and Gomez.

Gerald Ethridge Gomez was born of Portuguese stock at Belmont, Port of Spain, son of J. E. Gomez, who also played cricket for Trinidad. He represented Trinidad for twenty years (1937–56), and was a member of the West Indian touring party to India and Pakistan in 1948–49, and to Australia and New Zealand in 1951–52. He toured England in 1950. He managed the West Indies on their famous tour of Australia in 1960–61. The series drew huge crowds, including 90,000 in the fifth Test at Melbourne, with 500,000 people lining the streets to Melbourne airport.

It is a feature of West Indies cricket that the governance and administration of the game is very largely in the hands of the old players, and in this respect no one perhaps has served it better than Gomez. Starting as a batsman, he developed the skills of a medium-pace swing bowler. For many years he represented Trinidad on the West Indian Board of Control: he became a selector and, in that capacity, attended a Test in Guyana, where the appointed umpire fell ill. Gomez quickly donned the white coat. He also had a high reputation as a coach. His most valuable contribution was probably as founder and permanent head of the West Indies Umpires' Association. So passionately do West Indians regard their cricket that it is essential that there should be an organisation to safeguard their interests and to which officials should be responsible.

Gomez and Jeffrey Stollmeyer, a contemporary Trinidadian and boon companion, led parallel careers on the field and off until the latter's brutal murder in 1989. As youngsters they sat at the feet of the first great black West Indian batsman, George Headley. Together on the West Indian tour of 1948–49 they endured the rigours of travel on the Indian subcontinent soon after partition. They began as batsmen, Stollmeyer all slim elegance, Gomez square of jaw and rugged in physique and style. The latter, however, developed his bowling to the extent of sending down 729 overs in Indian heat, almost double the work-load of anyone else.

By 1950 in England, when West Indian cricket finally came of age with their victory in the Test series, the three famous Ws, all since knighted, Sir Clyde Walcott, Sir Everton Weekes and the late Sir Frank Worrell, were in full spate. Stollmeyer and Gomez were, however, not always overshadowed, the latter in Australia in 1951–52 heading both Test batting and bowling averages. Both in due course became efficient tour managers. When Worrell took West Indies again to Australia in 1960–61 for what was seen as a test of the black man's powers of leadership and turned out a triumph, starting with the tied Test and culminating in the ticker-tape farewell at Melbourne, he owed much to Gerry, his self-effacing, ever dependable manager and friend.

GEORGE HEADLEY

'The black Bradman'

Headley, George Alphonso, MBE   Professional

b: Colon, Panama, 30 May 1909   *Teams:* Jamaica, West Indies

Career batting:
103-164-22-9921-344*-69.86; hundreds 33-*ct* 76
Bowling: 1842-51-36.11

Test batting:
22-40-4-2190-270*-60.83; hundreds 10-*ct* 76
Bowling: 230-0

d: Meadowbridge, Kingston, Jamaica, 30 November 1983.
Aged 74.

George Alphonso Headley was the first great West Indian bats-man to make his mark on the Test scene, which he did in the last decade before the Second World War. George Challenor of Barbados had set the standard earlier in the eastern Caribbean, the islands of which had, however, little contact with Jamaica, a thousand miles away to the north. It was against the sides taken to Jamaica by the then Hon. Lionel Tennyson that this lithe little man, quick-footed and nimble of eye and brain, first showed his incomparable qualities. He was predominantly a back player with all the forcing strokes at his command, but when the ball was up to him he could drive with the best.

When the first Test series was played in the West Indies in 1929–30, he, only 20, scored 176 in his first Test against England, 114 and 112 in the third and finally 223 to save the match and the rubber in his home island. The West Indies were outplayed on their first trip to Australia in 1930–31, but his own reputation stood so high that he was forever in that country labelled 'the black Bradman'. In England in 1933 he carried West Indies, scoring 2,320 runs, more than twice as many as the next man, and averaging 55, again more than double the next average in the three-Test series.

When comparison is made between Headley and the other famous West Indian batsmen, it needs to be remembered that in his day he stood alone with little support. Sir Gary Sobers, Vivian Richards and the immortal trinity of Worrell, Weekes and Walcott, it may be said, rank with him in the same exalted company, but none could be rated his superior. On Headley's second visit to England in 1939 he made two hundreds in the Lord's Test match, in which the youthful Jeffrey Stollmeyer was the only other man on the side to reach 50. This is the performance still so widely remembered in this country.

The end to Headley's supremacy came with the war. When MCC returned to the West Indies in 1947–48 he was appointed captain in the first Test, the first black man to be so honoured. But after that he dropped out of the series with an injured back. He accompanied the West Indies side which immediately after partition made the first tour of India in 1948–49 but the rigours of travel and the heat were too much for a frail physique and he achieved little. His fellow Jamaicans even brought him back home by public subscription when MCC toured the West Indies in 1953–54, but at 44 he was only a shadow of the old self. In his prime Headley was a superb all-round fielder only less brilliant and spectacular than Learie Constantine. He could also bowl more than usefully both varieties of right-arm spin.

A quiet, singularly modest man, he was specially proud of the fact that his son Ron became a Test cricketer and fine opening bat for Worcestershire. Although he was born in Panama, George until his death remained Jamaica's favourite son.

JEFFREY STOLLMEYER
Devoted son of Trinidad

Stollmeyer, Jeffrey Baxter

b: Santa Cruz, Trinidad, 11 March 1921

Sch: Queen's Royal, Trinidad   *Teams:* Trinidad, West Indies

Career batting:
117-194-16-7942-324-44.61; hundreds 14-*ct* 93
Bowling: 2482-55-45.12

Test batting:
32-56-5-2159-160-42.33; hundreds 4-*ct* 20
Bowling: 507-13-39.00

d: Melbourne, Florida, USA, 10 September 1989. Aged 68.

Jeffrey Stollmeyer was a leading figure in the world of West Indian cricket for half a century. He had been flown to a Florida hospital after suffering multiple gun wounds from an attack by bandits in his home at Port of Spain, Trinidad. Aside from his cricket, Stollmeyer was a devoted son of Trinidad, active in public life as landowner and employer, parliamentarian and newspaper executive. He served as senator in the Trinidad Parliament after independence and at his death was chairman of the *Trinidad Guardian*.

Jeffrey Stollmeyer was the youngest of six sons of Albert Victor Stollmeyer. Most of his brothers migrated to America, although Victor played once for the West Indies. Rex spent much of his life in Canada, becoming trade commissioner there for Trinidad and also for the West Indian Federation. Jeffrey inherited the family coffee, cocoa and citrus estates at Santa Cruz outside Port of Spain and ran them for many years. He sold out and moved into the city largely on grounds of security.

Jeff Stollmeyer was an opening batsman of style and polish. He came first to England with the 1939 West Indian team at the age of 18, along with his nearest brother, Victor. Jeff made 59 at Lord's in his first Test innings and 59 also at The Oval, where Victor scored 96. After the war Jeff and John Goddard were the captains who first brought West Indian cricket to the front. He toured India and Australia in addition to coming again to England – along with the celebrated trinity of Walcott, Weekes and Worrell, and the spin partnership of Ramadhin and Valentine – in the victorious team of 1950, the first to succeed here against England's full strength.

Stollmeyer was the last white captain whose appointment went unquestioned in the West Indies. He advocated the promotion of Worrell (afterwards Sir Frank) five years before it happened; and in his memoirs, *Everything Under the Sun*, described Worrell being overlooked in 1954–55 when he himself was injured as 'a preposterous decision' by the white selectors.

Stollmeyer's first important work for the West Indies Board was as manager of the 1966 team to England which marked the start of Gary (afterwards Sir Garfield) Sobers's reign as captain. The tour was a great success, the turning point being a vast sixth wicket stand of 274 at Lord's between Sobers and his cousin David Holford when it seemed England had the game in their hands. That was the time when, on the fourth morning, the MCC Secretary was inclined to ring Buckingham Palace with the idea of bringing forward the Queen's visit that afternoon. Jeff suggested waiting for an hour to see how the game developed. The pair were still together 24 hours later when Sobers declared. The match was drawn.

Stollmeyer became president of the West Indies Board in 1974, and so was in office when the Australian Kerry Packer recruited many of the best cricketers, including most of the West Indies team, to his so-called 'World Series Cricket'. When the International Cricket Conference passed a resolution barring Packer's players from Test cricket the West Indies, disliking the retroactive principle implied, was the only ruling body to vote against the resolution which was afterwards overruled in the High Court. Stollmeyer leaves a widow, Sara, who was also wounded in the attack.

SIR FRANK WORRELL

Honoured at Westminster Abbey

Worrell, Sir Frank Mortimer Maglinne   Professional

b: Bank Hall, Bridgetown, Barbados, 1 August 1924

Sch: Combermere   *Teams:* Barbados, Jamaica, West Indies, Commonwealth

Career batting:
208-326-49-15025-308*-54.24; hundreds 39-*ct* 139
Bowling: 10115-349-28.98

Test batting:
51-87-9-3860-261-49.48; hundreds 9-*ct* 43
Bowling: 2672-69-38.72

d: Mona, Kingston, Jamaica, 13 March 1967. Aged 42.

Frank Worrell, who died with such tragic suddenness at the age of 42, will be remembered as a cricketer of the highest attainments, as a great captain and not least as an outstanding citizen of the West Indies. His cricket came to light in Barbados during the war years. He made 308 not out against Trinidad at the age of 19. When the West Indies re-entered the Test scene in 1948 he was a natural choice along with the other members of the trinity of 'Ws' from the same island, Clyde Walcott and Everton Weekes. Thereafter the achievements in concert of these three are legendary. Walcott and Weekes had, however, retired from Test cricket when at the age of 36 Worrell was faced with his sternest trial.

In 1960 he assumed the captaincy of the West Indies in Australia for what turned out to be in all respects the best, as well as the most exciting, series of modern times. The climax of it was a farewell motorcade through the Melbourne streets amid a cheering throng of half a million people. Three years later he led the

West Indies to their famous 1963 success in England. Announcing his retirement at the end of this tour, he was knighted the following year. By this time he had assumed high responsibilities, first with the University of the West Indies in Jamaica and then as a worker in social fields with the Trinidad Government.

However, he had one further contribution to make to West Indies cricket. When in 1965 Australia visited the Caribbean, Worrell undertook the management of the West Indies team, now under the captaincy of Garfield Sobers. Thus fortified and advised, Sobers led his men to success in the rubber. Thanks to the pair of them, for the first time the West Indies now indeed bestrode the cricket firmament as undisputed champions.

Worrell was a magnificent cricketer, as elegant a batsman as ever walked to the wicket, and on his day a dangerous bowler, but it was as a leader of serene temperament who commanded the loyalty and affection of his men to an extraordinary degree that his name will shine with a special lustre in the game's history. It was, of course, his high personal qualities which gave him such a valuable influence with young people. In the developing countries of the West Indies he seemed to have a special part to play and I believe nothing was more certain than that a Governor-Generalship would have been offered him had he lived to full maturity.

Worrell's rise as a cricketer, remarkable though it was, is simply the story of a man of much natural talent making the most of it. His development in the broader sense is even more interesting. As a young man he was considered too outspoken for the local cricket authorities of the day and on this account his services were not utilised for the first post-war West Indies tour, to India in 1948–49. Worrell, however, set his sights on other targets. He forthwith began a long career in the League, first with Radcliffe and latterly with Norton, making his home in Lancashire and when not pursuing his living as a cricketer preparing for his degree at Manchester University.

It was his experience of living in the north that made him such a strong anglophile and so generous a host to English visitors to the West Indies. He was a hero in Jamaica and also in Trinidad. Strangely and sadly, he was slightly less of one in his native Barbados, where there is so strong a pride of island. Frank was a federalist who saw the many diverse elements of the West Indies as a homogeneous whole. It was this outlook that led to his frowning on what he took to be the presumption of Barbados challenging the Rest of the World. Time no doubt would have brought a complete rapprochement, for he had bought land in Barbados with an eye to his distant retirement.

Turning back specifically to his cricket, only Sobers among his countrymen can exceed his all-round figures. He made nine Test hundreds, six of them against England, who almost invariably found him at his best. As a batsman he was conspicuously correct in method, his bat as near to the vertical as the stroke made possible. Sir Neville Cardus has written of another and earlier great batsman that he added a bloom to the orthodox. The same could be said of Worrell. He was slim and lissom, a stylist who could not do an ugly or ungainly thing in any department. It was common talk that he should have been made captain of the West Indies before he was, though in fact he had twice been offered the leadership but had put his university career first. When the chance came in Australia it was accepted by the rest of his side, if not by him, as a challenge to his race. The result was a personal triumph of character and a spontaneity of performance on the part of his team that will never be forgotten in Australia.

He was the first sportsman to be honoured with a thanksgiving service at Westminster Abbey.

5

GREAT AUSTRALIANS

JACK FINGLETON
Steady blade and a sharp wit

Fingleton, John Henry Webb, OBE   Amateur

b: Waverley, Sydney, New South Wales, 28 April 1908

Sch: Waverley Christian Brothers College   *Teams:* New South
                                              Wales, Australia

Career batting:
108-166-13-6816-167-44.54; hundreds 22-*ct* 81-*st* 4
Bowling: 54-2-27.00

Test batting:
18-29-1-1189-136-42.46; hundreds 5-*ct* 13

d: St Leonard's, Killara, Sydney, New South Wales, 22 November
1981. Aged 73.

John Henry Webb Fingleton was an Australian cricketer of Test
pedigree, and a writer of distinction who combined political
and sporting journalism, with chief emphasis on cricket. He also
broadcast on the game with rare perception and dry, antipodean
humour both on radio and television. Jack Fingleton was the
author of ten cricket books, ranging from *Brightly Fades the Don*,
the story of the all-conquering Australian tour of England of 1948,
to his autobiographical *Batting From Memory*. His most important
contribution to cricket history perhaps was *Cricket Crisis* the defin-
itive story of the Bodyline tour of 1932–33, told with conspicuous
fair-mindedness by one of the participants and principal victims.
Fingleton wisely waited until after the war to publish his version
of the row over English bowling tactics, which had threatened to
split the Commonwealth.

In 1936, he achieved a distinction then unparalleled of scoring
four hundreds in successive Test innings, three in South Africa
and one against England at Brisbane. The 346 made together by
Bradman and Fingleton in the New Year Test of 1936–37 is the fifth

highest stand ever in England–Australia matches. Having narrowly missed selection to England in 1934, he came with Don Bradman in 1938, and made 1,141 runs on the tour with four hundreds. He was a steady rather than a scintillating player, a foil to Bradman and other bright stars of his days. He was a fearless fielder at short-leg.

To younger generations he will be chiefly recalled as an astringent critic and a man of wit; as the implacable opponent of Packer; for having appeared on TV in a cloth cap; for having poured ashes over his head at the conclusion of a Test series; and for having uproariously taken over the Parkinson Show.

JACK GREGORY
Explosive with bat and ball

Gregory, Jack Morrison   Amateur

b: North Sydney, New South Wales, 14 August 1895

Sch: Sydney Church of England GS, Shore   *Teams:* New South Wales, Australia, AIF

Career batting:
129-173-18-5659-153-36.50; hundreds 13-*ct* 195
Bowling: 10580-504-20.99

Test batting:
24-34-3-1146-119-36.96; hundreds 2-*ct* 37
Bowling: 2648-85-31.15

d: Bega, New South Wales, 7 August 1973. Aged 77.

Jack Morrison Gregory is a legendary name in cricket, and was the most glamorous member of a famous Australian family. Gregory was primarily a fast bowler of fearsome aspect, with a full gallop to the wicket and a great leap immediately prior to delivery with a high arm from every inch of his 6ft 3½. As a left-handed forcing bat he made the fastest 100 in Test history (in 70 minutes at Johannesburg), and as a slip fielder once took the record number of 15 catches in a series. Fast bowler, hitter, out-standing fielder and withal a dark and handsome figure: this all added up to a presence on the field to which one can think of only one parallel, Keith Miller. Learie Constantine? Possibly in terms of attraction, but Gregory, though scarcely so dynamic in the field, was a more dangerous fast bowler and a very much more consis-tent bat.

Gregory was discovered not in Australia, but at Lord's by 'Plum' Warner when, as a member of the AIF, he was billeted there in the summer of 1918. Warner was quick to proclaim his promise, which began its fulfilment with the AIF side who toured England the following year. He stepped naturally into the 1920–21 series in Australia, in the third Test of which there began the famous fast-bowling partnership of Gregory and McDonald, the one all fury and effort, the other the embodiment of graceful, feline power. Gregory thundered over the turf, McDonald moved lightly and smoothly to the crease, scarcely making a mark.

There were divergent views as to who was the faster, but the combined impact was never in dispute. Australia won by large margins the first six Tests in which they played together before England recovered to the extent of drawing the last two of the home series of 1921. After that summer McDonald made his home here, playing first in the League for Nelson and then with great effect for Lancashire. Gregory toiled on without his contemporary's support for two more rubbers before he broke down with cartilage trouble in the first Test of 1928–29, and forthwith retired.

During the bodyline controversy of 1932–33 it was sometimes argued in defence of the English tactics that they were a continuation of those used by Gregory and McDonald. This was a serious injustice. Both knew the value of the short fast ball, but they used it as a variant, and never with a strong legside field which so greatly increased the menace of Larwood and Voce. Gregory gave a foretaste of what was to come when, in his second Test at Melbourne at the New Year of 1921, he made 100 in two and a quarter hours going in No. 9 and followed up by taking seven for 69 on an admittedly helpful wicket. He was at his best in those early post-war years, in that series taking 23 wickets at 24 runs each and averaging 77 with the bat.

LINDSAY HASSETT
'Puck in Flannels'

Hassett, Arthur Lindsay, MBE   Amateur

b: Geelong, Victoria, Australia, 28 August 1913

Sch: Geelong College   *Teams:* Victoria, Australia

Career batting:
216-322-32-16890-232-58.24; hundreds 59-*ct* 169
Bowling: 703-18-39.05

Test batting:
43-69-3-3073-198*-46.56; hundreds 10-*ct* 30
Bowling 78-0

d: New South Wales, Australia, 16 June 1993. Aged 79.

Lindsay Hassett succeeded Sir Donald Bradman as Australia's cricket captain in 1949, and held the post for a span of 24 Test matches until his retirement at the age of 40 after the tour of England in 1953. Although he inherited a powerful team, the departure of the man who had dominated Australian cricket for so long left a gap which could only have been satisfactorily filled by someone of exceptional qualities. The diminutive, soft-spoken Hassett proved that he possessed them. In his deceptively quiet way he exercised complete authority over his team, insisting upon the highest standards of sportsmanship on the field and friendly behaviour off it. He was the youngest of six sons of a real estate agent. At Geelong College he was a prodigy beyond the average, captain of cricket and football, and five years in the XI.

Hassett first came to outside notice when as a minute 17-year-old he made 147 not out for a Combined Victoria Country team against the touring West Indies. He was 23 before he commanded a regular place in the Victorian team, but a year later he came to England with Bradman's 1938 team, and so began a sequence of 43 Tests.

During the Second World War he served in Palestine and the Middle East. In 1945 he was made captain of the Australian Services team which toured first England (playing five 'Victory Tests'), then India, and finally the Australian states, before being demobilised. He became captain of Victoria in the 1946–47 season and remained so for the following six seasons, during which they twice won the Sheffield Shield. In retirement Hassett ran a sports goods store, reported Test cricket and soon became a regular, and conspicuously fair-minded, member of the ABC and BBC broadcast teams.

Cricket has always bred characters rich and rare and in any such gallery Hassett commands a place all his own. Ray Robinson called him 'Puck in Flannels'. He was 5ft 6 in – the height of Hanif Mohammad, and Willy Quaife of earlier days – an inch below his great contemporary, Neil Harvey. He showed in his cricket the inner toughness associated with his countrymen, yet could lighten the most tense moments with spontaneous humour.

In the 1948 Old Trafford Test the crowd showed their displeasure at some short fast bowling by Lindwall and Miller. Cyril Washbrook hooked high to long-leg where Hassett waited underneath just inside the boundary, and dropped the catch. A little later the same stroke was repeated and this normally impeccable fielder dropped it again. Whereupon he removed the helmet from the nearby policeman and held it upside down like an offertory bag: general laughter and the situation defused. In Lahore one very hot afternoon an Australian bowler left the field, returning only hours later when the tail-enders were in. Lindsay fiddled about, moving him, first a little one way, then the other, before finally motioning him back through the pavilion gate.

He batted in two contrasting styles divided by the war. In his early manhood he was a free, uninhibited stroke-maker – not only a brilliant cutter, hooker and glancer, befitting his size. By nimble footwork and precise timing he drove powerfully. He was the only man ever to hit separate hundreds in a match against the great O'Reilly, going down the pitch and repeatedly hitting over his head. He made a marvellous start to the England tour in 1938 with successive scores of 45, 146, 148 run out and 220 not out. His first major impact on the Test scene occurred in July at Headingley on a difficult wicket, in atrocious light, with a storm threatening and Bradman and McCabe just out. He went in at 61 for four; Australia needed another 44 to win the match and retain the Ashes, which they did; Hassett contributed a cool 33 in half an hour.

In 1945 he was a sergeant-major when appointed to lead the Australian Services team. He declined a commission, thereby confining himself to Service pay of 12 shillings a day, as against the 16s 6d for Pilot Officer Miller and his other officers. Considering that the team – which fulfilled nearly 50 fixtures involving almost continuous travel – brought back a love of cricket to crowds estimated at three-quarters of a million, the wage was a sparse recompense, although it appealed to the captain's whimsical humour.

When Australian Test cricket restarted in 1946–47, Bradman and Barnes were the only other survivors from the 1938 side. The need for a steadying hand was no doubt a factor in his decision to eliminate all risk from his batting. The touch was still there, the method flawless. Only the aggressive spirit was missing. An inexhaustible patience now brought him all his ten Test hundreds. Watching a stubborn innings from the Lord's press-box one day, he remarked: 'I'm glad I wasn't up here when I was down there.'

There was never a happier or more effective combination of captain and manager than that of Hassett and E. A. ('Chappie') Dwyer in South Africa in 1949–50. Hassett led Australia in 1950–51 to four victories before F. R. Brown's MCC side broke the monotonous post-war pattern by winning the last Test at Melbourne. The Ashes, after 18 years, at last changed hands in 1953 at The Oval where England won by eight wickets. Hassett's humorous speech of congratulation to the crowd thronging in front of the pavilion sealed an emotional moment. When, afterwards, an England selector said: 'Well done, Lindsay, that was perfect,' he replied with perhaps a hint of reproach: 'Yes, not bad considering Tony Lock threw us out.'

No Australian team exceeded this one in popularity, nor has any captain left behind warmer feelings of regard and affection. The only things that broke his composure were breaches of the rigid standards he observed himself and required of his men. In 1981–82 he bowed out of Test commentating, saying that he was fed up with players' misbehaviour. Lindsay's philosophy and that of too many of the moderns were oceans apart.

RAY LINDWALL
Rhythm and speed, the perfect model

Lindwall, Raymond Russell, MBE   Amateur

b: Mascot, Sydney, New South Wales, Australia, 3 October 1921

Sch: Darlinghurst Marist Brothers College, Sydney

Teams: New South Wales, Australia, Swanton to West Indies, International XI to Rhodesia, India and Pakistan

Career batting:
228-270-39-5042-134*-21.82; hundreds 5-*ct* 123
Bowling: 16956-794-21.35

Test batting:
61-84-13-1502-118-21.15; hundreds 2-*ct* 26
Bowling: 5251-228-23.03

d: Sydney, Australia, 22 July 1995. Aged 73.

Among the indisputably fast bowlers who have displayed their arts in Test cricket in modern times the name of Lindwall is at the top or very near it of every critic's list – and, assuredly, of every batsman who played against him. From the first paces of his run-up to the moment of his delivery and after it all was rhythm and beauty. The purist might only say that at the moment of the ball's release the arm might be higher, to which a response might be that the ball left his hand a shade more nearly over the stumps. The late out-swinger was, of course, his most deadly weapon, whether at a length drawing the batsman forward or as a yorker.

More and more as he matured as a Test cricketer he relied on the *threat* of extreme speed. He was a master of pace-change, slipping in the extra fast one occasionally; likewise the bouncer. By the time he toured England under Lindsay Hassett in 1953 he had another string to his bow, following one season of league cricket: out-swingers need good slip-fielders and it was when too many catches were going down that he practised and perfected the in-swinger aimed at the stumps.

Lindwall played first for New South Wales in 1941–42 just before the Japanese came into the war. He served with the Army in the jungles of New Guinea and had not been long home before the arrival of the MCC side of 1946–47. He was a very fit, unfledged 25 when England faced him first at Brisbane. His new ball partnership with Keith Miller was developed in that series, and it continued for five more. England had no effective answer to Australia's pace until Fred Trueman appeared with effect in the Ashes-winning fifth Test of 1953.

Lindwall was at his best on English turf and helped by English breezes. In both 1948 and 1953 he headed both the Test and first-class bowling averages. Twelve times in his 61 Tests he took five wickets or more in an innings. He was a more than useful bat when runs from him mattered. He hit two hundreds in Tests.

In 1954 he moved from Sydney up to Brisbane in order to cap-tain Queensland. He did not succeed in bringing Queensland their first Sheffield Shield. He was, however, not only rigorous in condemning anything affecting the spirit of the game but a good tactical thinker. When immediately after his retirement he returned to England on a press assignment, Richie Benaud, dur-ing the Old Trafford Test in 1961, consulted Ray as to whether he should exploit the then novel idea of bowling his leg-breaks from round the wicket into the bowlers' follow-through marks. He did so and snatched victory from imminent defeat. Benaud, as he wrote later, only resorted to it having had Lindwall's approval.

STAN McCABE

Fond cricketer

McCabe, Stanley Joseph   Amateur

b: Grenfell, New South Wales, Australia, 16 July 1910

Sch: St Joseph's College, Sydney   *Teams:* New South Wales,
Australia

Career batting:
182-262-20-11951-240-49.38; hundreds 29-*ct* 139
Bowling: 5362-159-33.72

Test batting:
39-62-5-2748-232-48.21; hundreds 6-*ct* 41
Bowling: 1543-36-42.86

d: Beauty Point, Mosman, Sydney, New South Wales, 25 August
1968. Aged 58.

For many at The Oval yesterday the talk turned sadly to Stan McCabe, whose death from an accident at the age of 58 was reported on Sunday from Sydney. For he was not only a magnificent cricketer by the standard of cold achievement, but one unmistakably cast in the heroic mould. His 232 against England at Trent Bridge in 1938, which Sir Donald Bradman said he would have been so proud to play, was one of the classic innings of history, and incidentally, in three and three-quarter hours, the second fastest double hundred in Tests. (Bradman in 1930 at Headingley takes the palm by a few minutes.) Even more thrilling maybe was the 187 not out, with which he scourged the English bodyline attack at Sydney in 1932–33. His hooking of the fast bowling that day is still spoken of with mystical reverence by those present. Perhaps equally skilful, though of a different kind, was his 189 not out on a broken wicket at Johannesburg in 1935–36.

Stocky, powerful, and with marvellously quick reflexes, he was perhaps happiest against speed, but he was equally well equipped to deal with all types of bowling, and one remembers the cool certainty with which, as a young man of 19, he helped Woodfull to steer Australia to victory against the spinners on a dusting Lord's wicket in 1930. He averaged 48 with the bat over 62 Test innings, and it is safe to say he would have made many more had they been really needed. For his values, like such of the truly great as Hobbs, Macartney, Woolley and others, were essentially qualitative. Going in number four after Woodfull, Ponsford and Bradman, I suppose he must have sat with his pads on longer than anyone before or since. Was there ever a more powerful batting quartet?

In an Australian era rich in spin but weak in speed, McCabe used to whip down a few brisk overs with the new ball, and not infrequently his nip off the pitch and late inswing brought him a wicket or two. In the field, he had the speed and strong arm of the born athlete, and indeed he came as near as any to one's conception of the perfect cricketer. In this respect he was perhaps the Australian counterpart to Walter Hammond. Like his famous contemporaries, Bradman and O'Reilly, he came to Sydney grade cricket from the country, all three having learned to play as boys on the concrete wickets of the Bush. Playing at a time when Anglo–Australian cricket relations were sometimes a good deal less than cordial, his cheerful and friendly personality was a point of contact between the two camps. Everyone who knew him was fond of 'Napper' McCabe.

ARTHUR MAILEY

Bohemian genius

Mailey, Arthur Alfred   Amateur

b: Zetland, Waterloo, Sydney, Australia, 3 January 1886

Sch: Waterloo State School, NSW   *Teams:* New South Wales,
Australia

Career batting:
158-186-62-1530-66-12.33; *ct* 157
Bowling: 18772-779-24.09

Test batting:
21-29-9-222-46*-11.10; *ct* 14
Bowling: 3358-99-33.91

d: Kirrawee, Sydney, New South Wales, 31 December 1967.
Aged 81.

Arthur Mailey, of New South Wales and Australia, was a great
leg-spin bowler of the 20s, the man who, complementing the
fast attack of Gregory and McDonald, helped first Armstrong and
then Collins to establish an era of ascendancy in their country's
cricket. In the series of 1920–21 he had 36 wickets, including nine
for 121 in the second innings of the fourth Test at Melbourne: both
were 'records' as regards Australian achievements against
England. But Arthur Mailey was a good deal more than a gifted
cricketer: he was a man of diverse and uncommon gifts, and as
such invites an unusual obituary.

When first chosen for Australia he was a labourer, and once
accepted to play in a Test though not truly fit. But his captain was
in the secret, won the match without using his bowling, and
Mailey was able to collect the match fee that meant much to him
without any awkward questions. Otherwise that tally of 36 would
no doubt have been higher. Mailey, self-taught, became both
writer and artist, whose whimsical and independent nature was

communicated equally by his pen and brush. Having taken all 10 wickets against Gloucestershire on the tour of Collins's team for a lucky number of runs, he called his autobiography *Ten for 66 and All That*. It is perhaps the best reminiscent book yet written by a cricketer. Though he could talk knowledgeably about the philosophy of spin bowling he never knuckled down seriously to criticism, amusing himself rather by advancing his theories of the moment which were directed generally against pompous administrators, stodgy batsmen and medium-paced bowlers, whom he thought boring. Writing for an evening paper, he once forecast an England Test team and forgot to include a wicketkeeper, and diverted the flood of letters by saying that the bowling was such that no keeper was necessary. Latterly he took to painting in oils and numbered Sir Robert Menzies as a patron as well as a friend. He was wont to travel in England in a small car with an easel in the boot, calling on friends both famous and obscure, and turning up at Australian matches or not, as the mood took him.

When, in failing health during the last MCC tour of Australia, he was reproached for not coming up to the first Test at Brisbane, he excused himself by saying: 'I make it a principle not to enter the State of which Mackay is a resident.' He no doubt liked Mackay as a man – who would not? – but deplored him as a cricketer. Mailey is the only bowler whom I have heard make the ball buzz as it left the hand – and that was in his sixties. He had a wonderfully rhythmical, rocking delivery from a wheeling action that began, so to speak, at the hip pocket. Probably no bowler in any age spun the ball more. He was a famous figure in some of the great sides of history: but it was as a man of kindly wit, solitary and romantic, a 'character' impossible to classify, that he will be affectionately remembered by the cricket world in which he moved for so long.

BILL O'REILLY

Hostile with the ball, scathing with the pen

O'Reilly, William Joseph, OBE   Amateur

b: White Cliffs, New South Wales, Australia, 20 December 1905

Sch: St Patrick's College, Goulburn   *Teams:* New South Wales, Australia

Career batting:
135-167-41-1655-56*-13.13; *ct* 65
Bowling: 12850-774-16.60

Test batting:
27-39-7-410-56*-12.81; *ct* 7
Bowling: 3254-144-22.59

d: Sutherland, Sydney, New South Wales, 6 October 1992. Aged 86.

The Australian, W. J. O'Reilly was, until Shane Warne came along, rated the most formidable of all leg-break bowlers. In 1999 the matter verges on the moot. O'Reilly played for Australia between 1931 and the outbreak of the Second World War. He also toured New Zealand in 1945–46. He reserved his best efforts for Tests against England, taking 102 wickets in 19 matches. Tall and gangling, he benefited from playing his early country cricket on concrete wickets, on which he could be 'almost unplayable' according to Sir Donald Bradman. When his playing days were over, O'Reilly the journalist remained an impassioned advocate of the declining craft of spin bowling. 'Just because Lillee and Thomson hit a few Poms on the head', he complained, 'we think we've got to win that way for ever.'

O'Reilly's fame rests on his appearance in only 27 Test matches, for he was 26 before he won his first cap and his skills were at their height when war came. He played one Test in New Zealand afterwards, but decided that at the age of 40 his legs could scarcely sustain his large, lumbering frame on hard Australian pitches and retired to the press-box. His pungent opinions enlivened the sports pages of the *Sydney Morning Herald* for more than 40 years. To describe his critical style as trenchant would be an understatement. When Kerry Packer attempted his take-over of world cricket in 1977 he found an implacable opponent in his fellow Sydney-sider. One-day cricket as played Down Under, with the coloured clothing and all the commercial ballyhoo attending it, was anathema to O'Reilly. While some temporised he saw that the primary object of the true game, to bowl out the other side, was being perverted into that of stopping them scoring, chiefly by an abundance of short, fast bowling.

Bill O'Reilly's name is inevitably closely linked with that of Sir Donald Bradman since before they came together into the State team they had been antagonists playing as country boys for their townships. When O'Reilly, a 20-year-old at a teacher-training college, first played for Wingello at Bowral in 1926, Bradman, three years his junior and already the local prodigy, scored 234 not out. O'Reilly could only console himself that he had had the boy wonder missed twice at slip and that he bowled him first ball when the game was continued the following weekend. From this cricket they both graduated in the Australian manner via Sydney clubs to the NSW XI.

Although O'Reilly was already a prolific wicket-taker his advance was much the slower, probably because the highly individual plunging action, front-on and knees bent, did not commend itself to the purists. Ian Peebles called it 'a glorious rampage of flailing arms and legs', from which emerged at a full slow-medium pace, and sometimes faster, every ball in a wrist-spinner's armoury, delivered with a rare degree of accuracy and an unusually high bounce. It was delivered, too, with a malignity of facial expression which inspired the nickname of 'the Tiger'. The genial side of his nature was well to the fore off the field, but on it he was a figure of rare hostility.

From his first appearance for Australia in 1931 O'Reilly dominated one Test after another, especially on English and South African pitches and when in harness with that other master of leg-spin, Clarrie Grimmett. Together in England in 1934, the pair of them took 53 Test wickets, subjecting English batsmanship to a protracted ordeal by spin. In South Africa over the Test series of 1935–36 their bag was 71.

O'Reilly was effective on any surface, for he seemed able always to induce those extra inches of bounce which made for such a rigorous examination in judgment of length and footwork. Even on the super-placid Oval pitch of 1938 on which Hutton made his record 364 and England declared at 903 for seven, he bowled 85 overs, conceding just two runs an over for three of the best wickets. His comments on that pitch remained splendidly lurid. On another pitch of consummate ease at Old Trafford in 1934 he had the wickets of Walters, Wyatt and Hammond in four balls, the last two clean bowled, and finished with seven for 189 out of a total of 627 for nine. When O'Reilly found a responsive English pitch – as at Trent Bridge in 1934 and Headingley in 1938 – he was too much even for the best. In the Headingley match his 10 for 122 combined with Bradman's third successive Test hundred on the ground to seal Australia's grip on the Ashes.

Bradman and O'Reilly were the dominant personalities of Australian cricket in the 1930s, poles apart temperamentally, but each wholly appreciative of the other's genius. Bradman has always named O'Reilly as the finest bowler he ever played.

When Bradman became captain of Australia for the visit of G. O. Allen's MCC team in 1936–37, the Australian Cricket Board, thinking that all was not well within the side, took the unusual step of reproving O'Reilly and four others of Irish ancestry for an alleged lack of co-operation. Bradman indignantly insisted that he had made no complaint, while O'Reilly was equally angry at this slur on his sportsmanship. He always gave 100 per cent, was hard but fair on the field, and later strongly condemned falling standards of behaviour. He was a free and easy left-hand bat who seldom bothered much about it, and, for his ponderous build, a safe performer in the field.

BILLY WOODFULL
The quiet Australian

Woodfull, William Maldon   Amateur

b: Maldon, Victoria, Australia, 22 August 1897

Teams: Victoria, Australia

Career batting:
174-245-39-13388-284-64.99; hundreds 49-*ct* 78
Bowling: 24-1-24.00

Test batting:
35-54-4-2300-161-46.00; hundreds 7-*ct* 7

d: Tweed Heads South, New South Wales, 11 August 1965.
Aged 67.

Billy Woodfull was a famous Australian cricketer of the inter-war time, an opening batsman who was nicknamed with good reason 'the unbowlable' and a successful Test captain. His average of 65 over his whole career has been exceeded by only the barest handful of the great batsmen: Bradman inevitably, Ponsford, his equally illustrious partner for Victoria and Australia, Headley of the West Indies, and Merchant, of India: that completes the list. I give this illuminating fact first because it stresses a quality not perhaps generally recognised. Woodfull was anything but a spectacular player. He used an extremely short back-lift, and presented an astonishingly placid front which bowlers found none the less frustrating when they recalled that after the blunting work was done, Bradman and McCabe were probably waiting keenly with their pads on.

If no one went into rhapsodies about Woodfull as a batsman, he equally failed to excite them as a captain. Yet his unassuming manner and quiet common sense served Australia wonderfully well in a difficult era of Test cricket. Only one other Australian before him, Joe Darling, had captained two Ashes-winning sides in England. In between the victories of 1930 and 1934 was the Bodyline tour of 1932–33 wherein Australia briefly lost the Ashes. For his calm demeanour in the torrid atmosphere of that disastrous episode the game of cricket was greatly in his debt.

Woodfull's appointment as captain of Australia for the 1930 tour of England, over the head of his state captain, J. S. Ryder, was a sensation in its day. He was given a young side whom few people expected to regain the Ashes held just previously by A. P. F. Chapman's team. That they did so owed much to this shy, quiet and most likeable schoolmaster. In England four years later, with the scars of the Bodyline row still fresh, his tact was of equal value, and the results from Australia's point of view similarly satisfactory.

The nearest he ever came to letting his feelings get the better of him was when he had been hit grievously over the heart by Larwood in the notorious Adelaide Test of 1932–33 and the MCC manager, in an atmosphere of general bitterness, ventured into the Australian dressing-room to express his sympathy. 'There are two sides out there, Mr Warner,' he said. 'And one of them is playing cricket.' When Woodfull retired from all first-class cricket after the 1934 tour, at the age of 37, he had led his country in 25 of the 35 Tests he had played in and had made seven Test hundreds, with an overall average of 46. But probably none of these hundreds could be matched with his second innings after injury in the Adelaide Test. When physical courage in an opening batsman and captain was never more needed, he carried his bat throughout for 73 out of the total of 193. Nothing could have expressed his character more fittingly.

6

HOUSEHOLD NAMES

KEN BARRINGTON
His life for cricket

Barrington, Kenneth Frank   Professional

b: Reading, Berkshire, 24 November 1930

Sch: Kakesgrove School, Reading   *Teams:* Surrey, MCC, England

Career batting:
533-831-136-31714-256-45.63; hundreds 76-*ct* 515
Bowling: 8907-273-32.62

Test batting:
82-131-15-6806-256-58.67; hundreds 20-*ct* 58
Bowling: 1300-29-44.82

d: Bridgetown, Barbados, 14 March 1981. Aged 50.

Ken Barrington died of a heart attack on the evening of a Test in Barbados when acting as Assistant Manager to the England team of 1980–81. The memory of him evokes an affectionate smile in all who knew him, for he was a transcendently friendly, sympathetic fellow, popular among his contemporaries, and after illness forced early retirement at the age of 38, a touring manager who established a singularly warm rapport with the next generation.

He was taken on to the Surrey staff at 18, but it was four years before he was first tried by the county and, though twice chosen for England in 1955, his period of outstanding success was the decade which ended with his reluctant decision to retire in 1968. In that time he played on eight winter Test tours besides holding up the Surrey and England batting every summer. He was an attractive free scorer in his youth, but saw his role as a saver of Tests rather than as a cavalier. His two-shouldered stance with the look of a boxer was a monument of resolution and his method eschewed all risk. On hard pitches abroad he was in his element:

of the 20 Test hundreds he made in those ten years 14 were on tour against the strongest countries. Occasionally he let himself go, notably in 1966 at Melbourne when he reached his hundred in 2½ hours. With Ted Dexter's 1962–63 side in Australia he averaged 80.

A few batsmen have averaged more in Tests than over their whole career but I doubt if anyone with 82 caps showed a greater disparity, 45 overall, 58 in Tests. The one thing which provoked him into protest was the over-use of short, fast bowling with obvious intimidatory intent, as practised by the West Indians.

Ken acted in three successive winters as Assistant Manager to England abroad, lastly with Alan Smith in the West Indies. He was much affected by the Guyana government's last-minute decision to expel Robin Jackman because of his South African connections, and England's consequent departure with the Georgetown Test unplayed. A heart attack in 1968 had caused his premature retirement as a player. From the second attack, a fortnight only after the traumatic events in Guyana, there was no recovery.

The TCCB were not slow to recognise and utilise Barrington's shining qualities. In 1975, unusually young, he was appointed a Test selector, and, following that, he was given the managerial role which saw him at his best.

DENIS COMPTON
Hero out to please

Compton, Denis Charles Scott, CBE   Professional

b: Hendon, Middlesex, 23 May 1918

Sch: Bell Lane School, Hendon   *Teams:* Middlesex, Holkar,
Europeans, MCC, England,
Commonwealth, Cavaliers

Career batting:
515-839-88-38942-300-51.85; hundreds 123-*ct* 416
Bowling: 20074-622-32.27

Test batting:
78-131-15-5807-278-50.06; hundreds 17-*ct* 49
Bowling: 1410-25-56.40

d: Windsor, Berkshire, 23 April 1997. Aged 78.

W hat marked Denis Compton's batting from the first was a
sense of enjoyment in it all, of risks taken and bowlers
teased, that at once communicated itself to the crowd. Yet, while it
was the liberties he sometimes took which were written and
talked about, when the need arose his defence could be as orthodox as anyone's.

He was only 20 when, in 1938, with all the poise and coolness
of an old hand he saved England from probable defeat against
Australia at Lord's in an innings of 76 not out. A fortnight earlier,
in his first Test against Australia at Trent Bridge on a perfect
wicket, he had made the fourth hundred of the innings, following
those of Barnett, Hutton and Paynter. But it was in the Lord's
game, on a pitch made awkward by rain, before that most dis-
criminating of crowds, that he buckled down to the job and
showed both the full range of his skill and the temperament to go
with it.

He had been chosen first for England in the third and last Test of the 1937 summer against New Zealand, making 65 before, as the non-striker, being run out from an accidental diversion by the bowler. That was pure ill-luck, but prophetic in that the one flaw in his batting was running between wickets. His great friend and partner, W. J. Edrich, is credited with the remark that Denis's initial call was no more than a basis for negotiation. This happy-go-lucky approach – banished only at the crease when things really mattered – occasionally tested the patience of his captains. Hence J. J. Warr's remark that Compton took 415 catches in the course of his career 'when he was looking'.

As might be expected, Compton did not thrive on leadership, either as vice-captain to F. R. Brown on the Australia tour of 1950–51 or with Middlesex when he and Edrich shared the captaincy in 1951 and 1952. He was too pressed in organising himself to relish the responsibility of looking after ten others. His personality was otherwise expressed. Good-looking and debonair, Compton was the idol of spectators everywhere, in Australia, South Africa and the West Indies, as well as at home. To a war-weary nation, aching for entertainment, he was the national 'pin-up', a hero dangerously exalted who was yet never spoiled. Compton was one of the first sportsmen for whom an agent was an urgent necessity, to cope not only with commercial approaches but cascading fan-mail.

The *annus mirabilis* was 1947 when he made 3,816 runs (easily topping Tom Hayward's record 3,518, made in 1906). His 18 hundreds that year exceeded the record 16 of Sir Jack Hobbs, made in 1925; his average was 90. It was a gloriously hot, dry summer during which the South Africans suffered most from his bat, to the tune of six hundreds, four of them in Tests. Compton, however, was never an accumulator for the sake of it; and it was only Middlesex's need for plenty of quick runs in their successful chase of the County Championship that sustained his appetite.

Perhaps his two greatest innings were those against Bradman's all-conquering Australians in 1948: 184 at Trent Bridge in an eerie, yellow light with Lindwall and Miller at their fastest, and 145 not out at Old Trafford. This was the time when, within a few minutes of going in, he was obliged to retire for stitches to a cut eyebrow, sustained in hooking at a no-ball from Lindwall. We saw now, in the words of Neville Cardus, the Ironside breastplate as well as the Cavalier plume. Bandaged but indomitable, he returned to play an innings which laid the foundation of what would likely have been an England victory had the weather not interfered. At this point, he had made eight hundreds in the last ten Tests, a sequence which only Bradman had achieved. But now, at his peak, an old football injury to Compton's right knee began to give out danger signals. For a while the surgeons and 'physios' contrived to keep him on the field, and in the spring of 1950, in his last game of football, with the knee heavily bandaged, he helped Arsenal to victory in the Cup Final. Within a few weeks he was hobbling off the field at Lord's, and W. E. Tucker, the famous orthopaedic surgeon, was performing the first of numerous operations, which culminated in 1955 with the removal of his kneecap.

In the tour of Australia in 1950–51, with English batting at its weakest, Compton had an utter failure, his only one in a Test series. He never touched again the brilliance of his golden period. Nevertheless, handicapped in mobility as he was, he was still an automatic choice for England, and in the following three rubbers against Australia was batting at the moment of victory. The Ashes were regained in 1953 and retained in 1954–55.

In 1956, at The Oval, shortly after a rigorous surgical manipulation and still with a limp, Compton faced the old enemy for the last time. Showing many glimpses of his best, he made 94, the highest score of the match, and 35 not out. Sir Donald Bradman described his 94 as the best innings of the series. The following winter Compton made his last MCC tour, to South Africa, and then announced that 1957 would be his final season. He made 1,554 runs that summer at an average of 34, and in the last match at Lord's showed his flair for the occasion by hitting the Worcestershire bowlers for a sparkling 143. Though scarcely an all-rounder in the Test sense, Compton, bowling slow left-arm, sometimes in the classical style, sometimes with wrist-spin, had days of high success. At The Oval in 1947 against Surrey he took 12 for 174 in addition to making 137 not out. In three successive summers he bowled 2,000 overs and took 208 wickets, besides scoring 36 hundreds. Against Australia in the fateful Test at Headingley in 1948, he would surely have won the day for England on a dusty pitch if Bradman (twice) and Morris had not been missed off his bowling early in their innings. As it was, they respectively made 173 not out and 182 out of the 404 for three, which brought victory, and the rubber, to Australia.

When one considers the loss of six wartime summers from the age of 21 onwards, and the later physical handicap, Compton's achievements, numerically speaking, are marvellous indeed. His 38,942 runs, including 123 hundreds, were made at an average of

51.85; his 5,807 Test runs, including 17 hundreds, at 50. His slow left-arm bowling yielded 622 rather expensive wickets.

Retiring before his 40th birthday, Compton made successful careers in advertising and in journalism with the *Sunday Express*, for which he wrote about cricket (generally not unaided) from 1950 to 1988. He also commentated over many years on television, often with unexpected force.

Denis Compton, who died on St George's Day after a long illness, had a son by his first wife, Doris Rich, a dancer, and two sons by his second, Valerie Platt. He married thirdly, in 1975, Christine Franklin Tobias; they had two daughters.

BILL EDRICH

Half of a great partnership

Edrich, William John, DFC   Amateur

b: Lingwood, Norfolk, 26 March 1916

Sch: Bracondale   *Teams:* Middlesex, MCC, England, Tennyson
to India, Howard to India

Career batting:
571-964-92-36965-267*-42.39; hundreds 86-*ct* 529-*st* 1
Bowling: 15956-479-33.31

Test batting:
39-63-2-2440-219-40.00; hundreds 6-*ct* 39
Bowling: 1693-41-41.29

d: Whitehill Court, Chesham, Buckinghamshire, 24 April 1986.
Aged 70.

B ill Edrich, who died suddenly during the night of 23–24 April
in his Hertfordshire home, unlike his great contemporary Jim
Laker, who died a few hours earlier, had suffered no previous ill-
health and had been in his usual robust form at a Middlesex pre-
season dinner at Lord's.

In all that he did on the field and in war Edrich was the person-
ification of determination and courage, the very epitome of 'guts'.
His name is coupled immortally, of course, with that of Denis
Compton in the Middlesex sides from 1937 until 1958 in one of the
most fruitful of all partnerships. Though Compton was as brave a
fighter as Edrich when it came to facing Miller and Lindwall, the
game came so much more easily to him than to his great friend,
and the obvious contrast in method and temperament was part of
the fascination to the public of their innumerable partnerships
together. Edrich was never a graceful player. He was a good cutter,
but with the bottom hand in control his most telling strokes were

the hook and the pulled drive. In a tight corner he was apt to over-come technical limitations with that indomitable spirit.

The Norfolk Edriches were and are steeped in the game, and at one time could raise a formidable family team. Three of Bill's brothers, G.A. and E.H. of Lancashire, B.R. of Kent and Glamorgan, played county cricket, and his cousin J.H. for England and Surrey. Bill opted for Middlesex, qualifying via the MCC ground staff, and when his days at Lord's were over he returned to his roots as captain of Norfolk, for whom he continued to play with all the old zest until the age of 55.

In his first Middlesex season of 1937 Bill scored 2,000 runs, as he was to do eight times more, the climax coming with 3,539 in 1947, a total exceeded only by Compton who in that same golden summer piled up 3,816. When in 1938 Edrich (W.J.) scored 1,000 runs (all at Lord's) before the end of May an early baptism in Test cricket was certain. It came with disastrous results, his six innings against Australia totalling 67 runs and his first five against South Africa the following winter only 21. Then in the second innings of the last Test at Durban (the 'Timeless' one which lasted ten days) he at last justified the confidence of his captain, Walter Hammond, by making a dogged 219.

As a squadron leader he won the DFC for daylight bombing over Germany, and at the war's end he resumed his cricket as an amateur. Then it was W. J. Edrich who in Australia in 1946–47 established himself as a cricketer of true Test stamp, at No 3 in the order and also in England's extremity as a fastish bowler pro-pelling that small, tough frame at the enemy as though his lungs would burst. Tests against Australia continued to bring the best out of him, his crowning moment perhaps being the innings of 55 not out which (with Compton at the other end) at last brought the Ashes back home at The Oval in 1953. His last Tests were played with Sir Leonard Hutton's winning team in Australia in 1954–55.

His time followed, after a short interval, an earlier palmy age of Middlesex cricket under F. T. Mann during which one Championship was won, one shared, and second place was achieved four times. In 1951 the partnership of Edrich and Compton jointly took over Middlesex from R. W. V. Robins, under whose bril-liant leadership they had been brought up. Captaincy, as also later committee work, was a sphere which came more naturally to Bill than to Denis, and the latter soon dropped out from the leadership in favour of his friend. Bill Edrich stood for all that was best in cricket: Lord's will not be the same without his cheerful presence.

WALTER HAMMOND
Most majestic since W.G.

Hammond, Walter Reginald   Amateur

b: Buckland, Dover, Kent, 19 June 1903

Sch: Portsmouth GS   *Teams:* Gloucestershire, South African
                          Air Force, MCC, England

Career batting:
634-1005-104-50551-336*-56.10; hundreds 167-*ct* 819-*st* 3
Bowling: 22389-732-30.58

Test batting:
85-140-16-7249-336*-58.45; hundreds 22-*ct* 110
Bowling: 3138-83-37.80

d: Kloof, Durban, South Africa, 1 July 1965. Aged 62.

The death of Walter Hammond came as a shock to those who, coming back from the MCC South African tour, reported how wonderfully he seemed to have recovered from a grievous car accident a few years ago, which must have proved fatal to one of a lesser constitution. He even took part with some of them in a one-day match which enabled the English party to catch a glimpse of the most majestic presence that graced a cricket field since 'W.G.'. The adjective is the hoariest of clichés but it is completely apt. There has been nothing like the calm serenity of Hammond advancing to the crease, and surveying the field after taking guard. If he made a duck he did so like an emperor, but of course, ducks were not his speciality. Between 1927 and 1947 (six years being lost by war) he made more runs in Test cricket than any other man: 7,249, averaging 58, and including more hundreds (22) than anyone bar Sir Donald Bradman. With 110 Test catches, most of them in the slips where he scarcely had a superior, he far and away headed the field. He was also a more than useful change bowler of about the pace of Maurice Tate, with, as might be supposed, an action that mirrored all the virtues. He was in fact, as may be imagined, a superb natural games-player who could make himself almost equally at home on the golf course, or on the squash and lawn tennis courts.

The basis of his batting was the massive power of his driving straight and to the off, but he used every stroke, except the hook to fast bowling. O'Reilly aimed to peg him by attacking his legs, but this only curbed his speed of scoring. He averaged 51 against Australia. In Test cricket he never played better than in his first Australian tour under A. P. F. Chapman when he scored the record aggregate of 905 with an average of 113. But the innings that will specially be remembered by English followers will be his masterful 240 against Australia at Lord's in 1938.

His first-class record was as imposing as his figures in Tests. With 50,551 runs to his name he had a higher aggregate than all save Hobbs, Woolley, Hendren, Mead and Grace, all of whose careers were substantially longer. His centuries, numbering 167, have been bettered only by Hobbs and Hendren. Only two men, Woolley and Grace, held more than his 819 catches. No one exceeded his 78 in a season, or his 10 in a match, achieved in 1928.

His unique value to Gloucestershire was never shown more scintillatingly than in a certain five days in the Cheltenham Festival of that year. In the same match against Surrey which contained the 10 catches, he made a hundred in each innings, 139 and 143. Next came Worcestershire, bowled out before lunch by Hammond, who took nine for 23, went in and made 80 and followed up with six more wickets to give his side victory by an innings in two days. His skill on bad wickets should be specially noted. One recalls an innings of more than a hundred against Sussex at Horsham after a thunderstorm when everyone else got out as soon as they reached the batting end. In 1946–47, at Brisbane after another and greater thunderstorm, he gave Australia an object lesson in batsmanship on a wicket where the ball lifted and turned in a way impossible to predict. His exceptional speed of reaction here stood him in marvellous stead.

Was there then no flaw, no Achilles heel, in this truly wonderful cricketer? Technically his batting was only less than excellent against the fastest bowling. He could be discomposed by a Constantine or a Larwood, although the innings which greatly helped to bring him to fame was one of much splendour against McDonald at Old Trafford. The only limitation concerns his captaincy. On changing status from professional to amateur in 1938 he became captain both of his county and of England but, in Test cricket at any rate, the glamour that surrounded his own cricket found no reflection in his leadership. He was in particular too much of an individualist to make a good touring captain, and the failure of the 1946–47 side in Australia, despite the warmest of post-war welcomes, and an abundance of surrounding goodwill, brought about his immediate retirement.

But if the end was thus clouded nothing could seriously dim the memory of one of the greatest cricketers who ever played for England.

'PATSY' HENDREN

For he's a jolly good fellow

Hendren, Elias Henry   Professional

b: Turnham Green, Middlesex, 5 February 1889

Sch: St Mary's, Acton   *Teams:* Middlesex, MCC, England

Career batting:
833-1300-166-57611-301*-50.80; hundreds 170-*ct* 754
Bowling: 2574-47-54.76

Test batting:
51-83-9-3525-205*-47.63; hundreds 7-*ct* 33
Bowling: 31-1-31.00

d: Tooting Bec, London, 4 October 1962. Aged 73.

It is probably safe to say that no more popular cricketer ever played than Hendren (christened Elias but popularly known as 'Patsy' and among his friends as Pat). His technical record with the bat between 1907 and 1937 was remarkable enough, with figures which rank only slightly behind those of Sir Jack Hobbs and Frank Woolley. But though his deeds for England and Middlesex can be read about in books, the statistics of his career convey no impression as to the kind of man he was.

His short figure, his happy and sometimes wistful smile, his most obvious likeableness, and his facility for enlivening even the most serious situation with some perfectly timed and never over-done piece of clowning – all these endeared him to everybody, as much as did his flashing square-cut, his favourite lofted on-' ' e, his powerful hook off the fast bowlers, and his nimble fool rk against the slow ones. Everywhere he went he was persona gratissima – in the West Indies the affection for him developed almost into a cult, West Indian streets and children being christened 'Patsy'.

Learie Constantine
(1901–1971)

Gerry Gomez (1919–1996)

George Headley (1909–1983)

Sir Frank Worrell
(1924–1967)

Jeffrey Stollmeyer (1921–1989)

Lindsay Hassett
(1913–1993)

Jack Gregory (1895–1973)

Jack Fingleton
(1908–1981)

Ray Lindwall
(1921–1995)

Stan McCabe (1910–1968)

Arthur Mailey (1886–1967)

Bill O'Reilly
(1905–1992)

Billy Woodfull (1897–1965)

Ken Barrington
(1930–1981)

Walter Hammond (1903–1965)

'Patsy' Hendren (1889–1962)

Denis Compton (1918–1997)

Bill Edrich (1916–1986)

Sir Jack Hobbs
(1882–1963)

POPPERFOTO

COURTESY MCC

Lord Home of the Hirsel
(1903–1995)

Colin Milburn
(1941–1990)

P. B. H. May (1929–1994)

POPPERFOTO

A. P. F. Chapman
(1900–1961)

Herbert Sutcliffe
(1894–1978)

Sir George Allen (1902–1989)

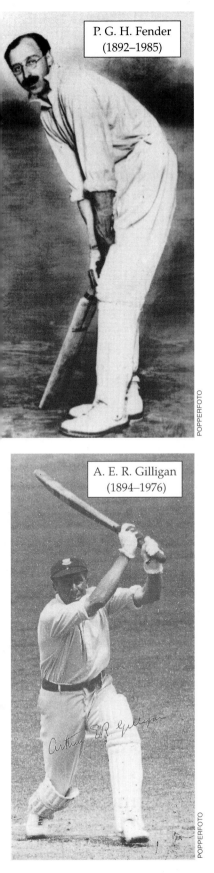

P. G. H. Fender
(1892–1985)

POPPERFOTO

A. E. R. Gilligan
(1894–1976)

POPPERFOTO

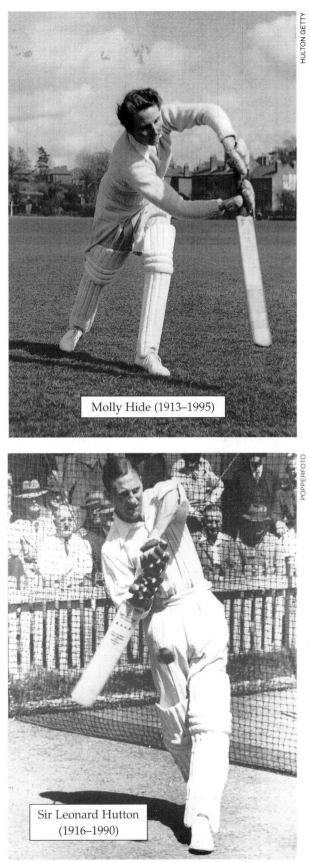

HULTON GETTY

Molly Hide (1913–1995)

POPPERFOTO

Sir Leonard Hutton
(1916–1990)

Brian Sellers (1907–1981)

Norman Yardley (1915–1989)

R. E. S. Wyatt
(1901–1995)

Wilf Wooller (1912–1997)

Nobody who was present will ever forget the scene, when, in his last match at Lord's in 1937, he scored his last hundred against Surrey. As soon as he got his hundredth run the crowd of some 17,000 rose to its feet and after repeated cheering sang 'For he's a jolly good fellow'. There has seldom been a more genuine tribute. Hendren did not burst with sudden brilliance on the cricket world. He was 24 when, after a long apprenticeship, he became indispensable to Middlesex. Only then began his famous association with J.W. Hearne – 'young Jack' – that meant so much to the county for so long. He was equally slow to develop as a Test cricketer, and until his middle thirties was in danger of being regarded as a first-rate county player rather than an essential part of the England XI. He was not the only one to fail against Gregory and McDonald, the Australian fast bowlers in 1921, but the parrot cry of 'temperament' arose.

A hundred against Australia at Lord's in 1926, and an even more valuable one at Brisbane for A. P. F. Chapman's team in 1928, showed how wrong his detractors were, and he became indispensable to England too. As a member of a touring side his personality counted for almost as much as did his performance on the field. Among his great feats may be mentioned his 301, not out, for Middlesex against Worcestershire in 1933, the scoring of more than 2,000 runs in every season between 1920 and 1929, including a total of 3,311 in 1928, a third-wicket partnership of 375 with Hearne, his colleague in many a productive stand, against Hampshire in 1923, and his 206 at Trent Bridge in 1925, when Middlesex, who were set to make 502, got the runs in six and a quarter hours. Hendren and F. T. Mann hit off the last 271 in 195 minutes.

In his prime he was among the best of outfields, and later became as adept at short-leg, where his work on the 1928–29 tour in Australia was invaluable. His opinion on any matter was always worth asking, and the younger Middlesex professionals, especially Compton and Edrich, owed much to his advice and guidance. In his last playing years he was an invaluable lieutenant to the youthful R.W.V. Robins.

His own contribution to the 'bodyline' controversy was the typical one of providing himself with a specially-made helmet, which he occasionally wore at Lord's when the wicket was bumpy. When he retired from first-class cricket in 1937, at the age of 48, he was appointed coach at Harrow in succession to Wilfred Rhodes. In 1939 Harrow beat Eton for the first time since 1908, and in the rejoicings afterwards Hendren was called out to the balcony and cheered again by the Lord's crowd. He retired from Harrow in 1947 and was first coach to Sussex and then scorer with Middlesex until 1959.

In his younger days he was a good Association footballer, and as outside-right for Brentford played for England against Wales in the 1919 'Victory' series.

SIR JACK HOBBS
The head of his profession

Hobbs, Sir John Berry   Professional

b: Cambridge, 16 December 1882

Sch: York Street Boys' School   *Teams:* Surrey, MCC, England, Vizianagram's XI to India and Ceylon

Career batting:
834-1325-107-61760-316*-50.70; hundreds 199-*ct* 340
Bowling: 2704-108-25.04

Test batting:
61-102-7-5410-211-56.94; hundreds 15-*ct* 17
Bowling: 165-1-165.00

d: Hove, Sussex, 21 December 1963. Aged 81.

Sir Jack Hobbs was the greatest English batsman since W. G. Grace, a supreme master of his craft, and the undisputed head of his profession. The son of the groundsman at Jesus College, Cambridge, he made his way to The Oval at the age of 20. Half a century later, long after his retirement, but when his name was still a household word, he accepted the honour of knighthood. Hobbs learned his cricket, as so many Cambridge men have done before and since, on that sublime stretch between Fenner's and the Town, called Parker's Piece. Tom Hayward was his mentor there, and it was Hobbs's luck, after Hayward had persuaded him to qualify for Surrey, that he should serve his apprenticeship at The Oval as opening partner to that great batsman.

There have been three men, as one surveys the history of cricket as a whole, whose genius and influence have transcended all others: W. G. Grace, Jack Hobbs and Don Bradman. Like most of the truly great – it was the same with Hutton and Compton,

Hammond and Woolley – Hobbs proclaimed his promise beyond all argument right away. He made 155 in his second match for Surrey, scored 1,300 in this first season of 1905 and improved considerably on that in his second. The next year he was chosen for the Players and also won a place in the MCC side to Australia of 1907–8. It was then already said of him that there was no better professional batsman in England bar Hayward and Johnny Tyldesley.

It was the second of his five visits as a player to Australia that brought him right to the top of the tree. In that series he averaged 82, scored three Test hundreds and with Wilfred Rhodes made 323, which is still the longest opening partnership for England against Australia. Noting the consistency of his scoring and the speed with which the runs generally came in those days, one can appreciate the remark of Frank Woolley's: 'They can say what they like about him, but only those of us who saw Jack before 1914 knew him at his very best.' However that may be, he was and remained the world's premier batsman until, when nearer 50 than 40, his gradual decline coincided with the advent of Bradman.

The long span of Hobbs's career made it probable that he would corner most of the aggregate records. Thus no one can match his number of runs, 61,221, any more than they can compete with his 197 hundreds. No doubt he was lucky with his opening partners – compared with, say, Hutton. Nevertheless, his figure of 166 stands of a century or more for the first wicket sets an almost unassailable target. Even more conclusive may seem the consistency of his performances. He averaged just under 50 in England over his whole time, stretching from 1905 to 1934. In Australia his average was 51, in South Africa 68, and in Tests alone it stood at 56.94.

Hobbs had two great Surrey partners, Hayward and Sandham, two even more famous for England, Rhodes and Sutcliffe. It was he and Sutcliffe who decided the Oval Test of 1926 that brought back the Ashes, after many crushing defeats, by their wonderful partnership of 172 on a bad wicket. In the next series in Australia these two paved the way to the victory that kept the Ashes safe by scoring 105 together on a Melbourne glue-pot – one of the classics of bad-wicket batsmanship. On A. E. R. Gilligan's tour of 1924–25 Hobbs and Sutcliffe, going in against a score of 600, batted the entire day for 283. If one summer marked his peak it was perhaps 1925, when, at the age of 42, he scored 3,000 runs, including 16 centuries, and with two hundreds in the match against Somerset at Taunton, first equalled and then surpassed the 126 hundreds made by 'W. G.'.

Early recollections of Hobbs are confined in my own case to inessential things like the frequent spinning of the bat in his fingers before he settled into his stance, and the way he pulled down the peak of his cap, so that it slanted almost parallel with his slightly beaky nose. Before I knew enough to admire his batting it was his fielding which fascinated most. He would walk about at cover in an innocent, preoccupied sort of way in between times, hands often deep in pockets. If the ball were pushed wide of him, and the batsmen made to run, he would usually move at quite leisurely speed to cut it off. Then suddenly an apparently identical stroke would be repeated and this time the relaxed figure would spring into action with catlike swiftness – there was a dart, a swoop, and the quickest of flicks straight at the stumps, with the batsman pounding to the crease as if for dear life. Australians as a rule are good between the wickets, but on one tour Hobbs at cover point ran out upwards of a dozen of them.

It has been written of him often enough that he was the bridge between the old batting and the new. When he entered the scene it was the age of elegance, and the best professionals absorbed and were caught up in the classical style based on the swing of the bat from the shoulders, driving, and the off-side strokes. There were, of course, strong on-side players, notably Fry, and more and more men came to practise the art of working the ball to the on-side. Hobbs was quickly identified with this school. Then, when he was still climbing to the top, came the revolution in technique that was made necessary by the arrival of the googly and the advance of the leg-spinner. At the same time the faster bowlers were exploring the possibilities of swing.

Neville Cardus has described Hobbs as 'the first batsman really to master the new bowling'. He combines with the classic freedom of forward play and full swing of the bat the necessary adaptation to defeat the googly and late swerve – legs and pads in front of the wicket with the hands held loosely on the bat in order to scotch the spin and bring the ball down short of the close fieldsmen, virtually in the crease.

But enough of technique. In the last resort the difference between talent and mastery is a matter of character. Hobbs brought to his cricket an ascetic self-discipline which in tight corners expressed itself perfectly in his play. He was a man of conspicuous personal modesty; but his pride in his position as – in every sense – England's No. 1 gave to his batting an aura of serenity equally communicable to his opponents and to his fellows. No one ever saw Hobbs rattled or in a hurry. And if he was anxious it never showed. There was a quiet dignity about him which had its roots in mutual respect: for others as for himself. He had the natural good manners of a Christian and a sportsman, and the esteem in which, in his day, his profession came to be held owed much to the man who for the best part of a quarter of a century was its undisputed leader.

LORD HOME OF THE HIRSEL

Cricketing Prime Minister

Home of the Hirsel, Lord, KT   Amateur

b: Westminster, London, 2 July 1903

Sch: Eton   *Teams:* Middlesex, Oxford U., MCC

Career batting:
10-15-6-147-37*-16.33; *ct* 9
Bowling: 363-12-30.25

d: The Hirsel, Scotland, 9 October 1995. Aged 92.

Lord Home of the Hirsel as Viscount Dunglass was a successful schoolboy cricketer at Eton. The only Prime Minister to have played first-class cricket, he came within distance of a blue at Oxford in 1926, had a couple of games for Middlesex, and in 1926–27 accompanied the MCC team which Plum Warner took to South America.

As a member of the powerful Eton XI of 1921, six of whom afterwards played first-class cricket, he played his part in the two emphatic victories over Harrow and Winchester. The Winchester match was the famous one wherein J.L. Guise made 278 (still the record score in an English schools' match) and yet was on the losing side. Thereby hangs a tale with which Alec Home and Gubby Allen for ever taunted one another. When Winchester, having been bowled out for 57, batted again 198 runs behind, Allen bowled the first ball to Guise, who snicked it. Still putting his gloves, on, M. L. Hill, the 'keeper, left the ball to Home at first slip, through whose fingers it went for four. The initial blame, maintained first slip, was the bowler's for delivering before the field was ready. Guise went on, hour after hour, in extreme heat until he was run out, whereupon it needed a dashing hundred by Ronny Aird to bring victory to Eton. At Lord's against Harrow in 1922, after a blank first day Dunglass made top score of 66 and took four for 37, thereby earning himself a place in the representative match, Lord's Schools v. The Rest. It was as a fast-medium bowler and middle-order bat that he was tried both for Middlesex and Oxford. After the MCC tour, which took in Uruguay, Chile and Peru as well as the Argentine, his cricket increasingly gave way to politics.

In 1966 Sir Alec Douglas-Home (during his Prime Ministership in 1963–4, having foregone his hereditary title) became President of MCC, the club thus having the advantage of his diplomatic qualities in the preparations prior to the devolution of power to the Cricket Council and through that new body to the TCCB and NCA. In 1971, freshly ennobled on becoming Tory leader of the House of Lords, he succeeded the 10th Viscount Cobham as Governor of I Zingari. He retained a keen interest in IZ cricket and the club's affairs until in his 80th year he handed on the mantle to F. G. Mann.

It could surely be said of Alec Home – the rarest of tributes to a man who had spent his life in public service – that he never had an enemy. To his kindness and consideration I owed a special debt. He not only wrote a delightful foreword to my biography of Gubby Allen and, incidentally, provided the subtitle *Man of Cricket*; at his suggestion he read and checked every page of the text.

P. B. H. MAY

Best of his time

May, Peter Barker Howard, CBE   Amateur

b: The Mount, Reading, Berkshire, 31 December 1929

Sch: Charterhouse   *Teams:* Surrey, Cambridge U., MCC, England

Career batting:
388-618-77-27592-285*-51.00; hundreds 85-*ct* 282
Bowling: 49-0

Test batting:
66-106-9-4537-285*-46.77; hundreds 13-*ct* 42

d: Liphook, Hampshire, 27 December 1994. Aged 65.

Peter May was a distinguished England captain and one of the finest batsmen since the Second World War. From 1951 when, as a Cambridge undergraduate, he made a hundred in his first Test match until his retirement from the game in 1962, May's batting for Surrey and England was beyond reproach. With the exemplary technique and unwavering application which characterised all the best English batsmen of his time, May was an outstanding performer in the classical amateur tradition. Six foot in height, broad in the shoulders and long in the leg, May always played with a perfectly straight bat. His trademark as a batsman was his superb style and strength when driving off the front foot through mid-on; but he had all the strokes.

May was a great admirer of Sir Leonard ('Len') Hutton, whom he succeeded as captain of England in 1955. Like Hutton, he was a thoughtful and sound, rather than exciting, leader, and was at all times conspicuously considerate towards the members of his team. When May joined the side, England's fortunes were already on the turn. From 1951 to 1958 the team contested eleven successive rubbers without defeat, winning eight and halving three. Of these Brown won one, Hutton three and May four. It was not all one-way traffic, though, and under May's leadership England lost twice to Australia.

Batting in the first half of his Test career at No. 3 and in the latter half at No. 4, May was the picture of unruffled composure, taking crises in his stride. In his 66 Tests, of which he was captain for 41, he made 13 hundreds and scored more than 50 (four times in the nineties) in another 22 innings. His figures are remarkable considering that he played for fewer than 12 seasons. As it chanced, May missed by a year the counties' adoption of one-day cricket. Although he was admirably equipped for any variation in the game, calling on May to play limited-overs cricket would, in J. J. Warr's words, have been 'like asking Sir Thomas Beecham to conduct the Rolling Stones'.

Peter May was educated at Charterhouse, where he enjoyed four highly productive years in the First XI. It would have been five but for Robert Birley, the headmaster, who ruled that at 13 he was too young. His first mentor was George Geary, a fine bowler between the wars and the cricket coach. In his autobiography May quotes the Geary gospel, which he aimed always to follow: 'Keep your head still. Stand still as long as you can. When you move your feet, move quickly, but the longer you stand still the later you'll play the shot.'

May did his National Service as a Writer in the Royal Navy, which he represented at cricket, before going up in 1949 to Pembroke College, Cambridge, where he read History and Economics. In the first year he picked up a soccer blue (later becoming captain), before playing against Oxford at Lord's for three successive summers. From the outset May was a heavy run-maker for both Cambridge and Surrey; during his second university year, in 1951, he scored a chanceless 138 on his Test debut, against South Africa at Headingley. Strangely, however, he failed to come off in the University match. Perhaps as a consequence David Sheppard, later Bishop of Liverpool, was preferred to him as captain in 1952.

It took May a while to make his mark against the touring Australians in 1953. After failing in his only innings in the first Test he was dropped – for the first and last time in his life. Brought back for the final Test at The Oval, May played an effective part in the victory which won the Ashes – formerly held by Australia for nearly 20 years. Thereafter he gave heart and sinew to England's sometimes fragile batting for 52 successive Tests, and played in several more after his career was twice interrupted by illness. In 1955, in his first series as captain, England narrowly beat South Africa, with May averaging 72. In 1956 May's side retained the Ashes, and his average was 90. In 1957, when England beat the West Indies three-nil, it was 97. As England captain he won 20 Tests (an unsurpassed record), lost 10 and drew 11.

At Edgbaston in the 1957 series May and Colin Cowdrey built the largest fourth-wicket stand in Test history (and the highest by England for any wicket): 288 runs behind after the first innings and forced to follow on, the English pair put on an astonishing 411. Unsure of picking Ramadhin's spin, May and Cowdrey pushed forward for hour after hour, using the front pad as a second line of defence. As an exercise in stamina and concentration the partnership was unique of its kind. May, who occupied the crease for just short of ten hours, was 285 not out – the highest score of his career. Cowdrey's share of the runs was 154. May may have set another record in 1957. Not by nature a convivial person, he nevertheless attended and spoke at 75 dinners in the course of the year. As captain of Surrey and England, May regarded it as part of his job to be an ambassador for the game. He was always guided by a strong sense of duty and so was especially wounded by the crude media criticism of his conduct as chairman of selectors.

His three overseas tours to South Africa, Australia and the West Indies were less happy for May than the home series of the 1950s. On the South African tour he amassed 1,270 runs, but in the Tests only once passed 50; after much stodgy cricket all round, the rubber was halved. In Australia in the winter of 1958 England faced several bowlers whose suspect actions went unpenalised. May held the batting together with Cowdrey, and bore the frustration with characteristic silence. But the team's morale suffered and Australia regained the Ashes with ease.

May missed half the 1959 season through illness, and his health again failed in the West Indies that winter, although not before England had handsomely won the only completed Test of the series. Unfit for all of 1960, May was persuaded to lead England against Australia once more in 1961. After his powerful first innings of 95 had put England in a commanding position in the fourth Test at Old Trafford, England collapsed on the final day, missing a golden opportunity to recapture the Ashes. On the county scene May led Surrey to the last two of their seven successive championships in 1957 and 1958; he remained as captain until his retirement at the end of 1962.

May then pursued a business career as an insurance broker and underwriter at Lloyds, chiefly with Willis Corroon. But he also played a full part at Lord's, first as a member of the England Selection Committee for four years and then, from 1982 to 1988, as its chairman. He also chaired at different times the TCCB and MCC cricket sub-committees.

From 1980 to 1981 May was a charming yet firm and decisive president of MCC. In 1985, in association with Michael Melford, he published his memoirs, *A Game Enjoyed*. An active member of the Surrey committee, May was due to be president of the club in 1995, its 150th anniversary year.

May married, in 1959, Virginia, daughter of the Sussex and England captain A. H. H. Gilligan; they had four daughters, all talented horsewomen.

COLIN MILBURN

Short and sweet

Milburn, Colin   Professional

b: Burnopfield, County Durham, 23 October 1941

Sch: Annfield Plain Secondary Modern and Stanley GS

Teams: Northamptonshire, Western Australia, MCC, England

Career batting:
255-435-34-13262-243-33.07; hundreds 23-ct 224
Bowling: 3171-99-32.03

Test batting:
9-16-2-654-139-46.71; hundreds 2-*ct* 7

d: Newton Aycliffe, County Durham, 28 February 1990. Aged 48.

Colin Milburn's was indeed an ill-fated life, first ruined in the cricket sense by the loss of an eye in a motor accident when, still in his 20s, he was rising swiftly to fame, and ended by his premature death at the age of 48. Milburn came from Burnopfield, near Newcastle, where his father Jack played as a professional in the Tyneside Senior League. Coming south to Northamptonshire, like other Durham men before and after him, he made a swift impact. His short, strong, chunky form, his smiling face and the uninhibited freedom of his play created a memorable impression in the often colourless cricket of the 1960s. His approach to batting enthused the crowds as scarcely anyone else's did, apart from Ted Dexter. In 1966 and 1967 he won the Lawrence Trophy for the fastest 100 of the season.

By now he was a successful Test cricketer, scoring 94 in 2½ hours on his first appearance, against West Indies in a losing cause at Old Trafford, and 126 not out in the following Test at Lord's. This effort, made out of 197 for four, which threatened at one point to win the match, showed him to have an orthodox defence in addition to the formidable power of stroke. In two seasons he did great things for Western Australia, headed by an unforgettable innings of 243 at Perth against Queensland of which 181 came in two hours between lunch and tea – a rate of scoring to which there are few parallels. At Lord's in 1968, against Australia, he took a rare battering on a lively pitch while making 83 in a match wherein England were robbed by rain.

Those two Lord's innings remain the jewel in the crown. Less than a year after the second of them came the road accident which destroyed his left eye, and also affected the right. A few years later he made a game effort to return to county cricket but, with the leading eye useless, the handicap was too great. In recent years Milburn was heard frequently as a BBC Test commentator. Nothing profound issued but good humour and earthy common sense. Showing the same qualities, he also made a popular reputation as an after-dinner speaker.

HERBERT SUTCLIFFE
Imperturbable for England and Yorkshire

Sutcliffe, Herbert   Professional

b: Summerbridge, Harrogate, Yorkshire, 24 November 1894

Teams: Yorkshire, MCC, England, Vizianagram to India and Ceylon

Career batting:
754-1098-124-50670-313-52.02; hundreds 151-*ct* 473
Bowling: 563-14-40.21

Test batting:
54-84-9-4555-194-60.73; hundreds 16-*ct* 23

d: Cross Hills, Yorkshire, 22 January 1978. Aged 83.

Herbert Sutcliffe, the Yorkshire and England batsman, was opening partner for county and country to Percy Holmes and Sir Jack Hobbs respectively. His career from the moment of his entry into the Yorkshire XI in 1919 was a success story almost without the suspicion of a break. He scored 1,839 runs in his first year, headed the county averages and forthwith established himself with Holmes in a first-wicket partnership which in the following fifteen years broke all records.

In his first Test (in 1924 against South Africa) Sutcliffe helped Hobbs, the greatest batsman of the day, in an opening stand of 136. In his next – and his first at Lord's – he made the first of his 16 hundreds for England. The following winter in Australia with MCC he had the best figures on either side, averaging 80 in the Tests. At Melbourne in one of the classic stands of history he and Hobbs batted all day for 283.

When England at last regained the Ashes at The Oval in 1926 it was an even more remarkable partnership of 172 with Hobbs on a most difficult wicket that settled the issue. Of all his innings Sutcliffe was proudest of his 161 on that momentous day. He was twice after that on the winning side with MCC in Australia. Between 1928 and 1932 he three times topped 3,000 runs. Against Essex at Leyton he made the highest score of his life, 313, in the partnership with Holmes that broke all records – 555 for the first wicket.

What a monument of achievement! Yet when contemporaries and critics discuss Herbert Sutcliffe in the context of the other great names of history they do so generally on a note of qualification. The fact is he was the perfect second string, the subsidiary in a technical sense not only to Hobbs, 'the perfect batsman', but also to the more brilliant and likewise more mercurial Holmes. Sutcliffe was a good cutter and a brave, if upward hooker. Gripping the bat with the face unusually open he habitually played the off-side ball square of the direction expected. You could not say that he was a master of all strokes, but he used what he had to the maximum purpose. He was a master of the short push for one, and there have never been two such judges of a single as Hobbs and Sutcliffe. Their understanding was so complete that they seldom even needed to hurry.

The foundation of Sutcliffe's cricket was a wealth of determination and concentration and an imperturbable calm. His black hair gleaming in the sun, legs crossed in an aloof, superbly confident manner when at the non-striker's end, he epitomised self-confidence and good sense. So it was in his personal life. One of the long string of Yorkshire cricketers deriving from Pudsey, he was about to blossom on the county scene at the outbreak of the 1914–18 war, during which he rose from the ranks, finishing as a captain in the Yorkshire Regiment.

Playing in an age in which professional captaincy was almost non-existent, he once, with the height of dignity, declined the leadership of Yorkshire. On his retirement at the age of 44 he became a successful man of business. He served many years on the Yorkshire committee, became rather late in life a Test selector, and was President of the Forty Club. The high repute of the professional cricketers of his day as sportsmen and gentlemen in the truest sense owed much to the example of such men as he.

7

SOME CAPTAINS

SIR GEORGE ALLEN

'Wedded to cricket, the power at Lord's'

Allen, Sir George Oswald Browning, CBE   Amateur

b: Bellevue Hill, Sydney, NSW 31 July 1902

Sch: Eton   *Teams:* Middlesex, Cambridge U., MCC, England

Career batting:
265-376-54-9232-180-28.67; hundreds 11-*ct* 131
Bowling: 17518-788-22.23

Test batting:
25-33-2-750-122-24.19; hundreds 1-*ct* 20
Bowling: 2379-81-29.37

d: St John's Wood, London, 29 November 1989. Aged 87.

Sir George Allen, universally known as 'Gubby', had a stronger influence on the world of cricket and for a longer span of years than anyone since the 4th Lord Harris. Allen played the first of his 25 Tests in 1930. He captained England both at home and in Australia; was elected to the committee of MCC in his early thirties; and served the club as both treasurer and president, as well as on successive committees for more than 50 years. Harris, who led England in the first Test in this country in 1880 and was a dominating influence in the game until his death in 1932, had trodden all these paths, and when it came to mastery of argument on important issues those who sat in committee with both probably accorded them equal attention and respect.

George Oswald Browning Allen was born in Sydney on 31 July 1902, of a family with deep roots in Australia. His great-grandfather emigrated in 1816, was the first man in Australia to serve his articles as a solicitor there, and founded what today is the oldest legal firm in Sydney. Gubby's father, Walter, brought his family to England in 1909, and at the outbreak of the 1914–18 war joined the Metropolitan Special Constabulary, eventually becoming Commissioner and earning a knighthood. From his private schooldays at Summerfields, Oxford, young Allen showed that he had cricket in the blood. An uncle had played for Australia and it was said his father might have played for Cambridge in the era of Ranji and Stanley Jackson if he had exerted himself rather more. That was a charge which could never have been made against his son.

When Eton and Harrow resumed their rivalry at Lord's in 1919, Allen was run out in the first over on the first morning without receiving a ball. However, things turned out well for him — as they generally did — in the second innings, his 69 not out helping Eton to an easy victory. He was lucky in having for a housemaster C. M. Wells, formerly of Cambridge and Middlesex, who ran the cricket, and for a coach the celebrated George Hirst. By the time their mettlesome protégé left Eton, his promise as a fast bowler, with a beautiful action and late out-swing, was clearly recognisable. He was correct and determined as a batsman. Allen walked into Hubert Ashton's powerful Cambridge side of 1922 and his nine wickets in the University match for 78 runs sped Oxford to an innings defeat.

After two years he left Cambridge for the City, where he developed into a successful stockbroker, and thereafter became his own brand of amateur, playing never even half a season for Middlesex and, despite this, reaching the top of the tree as an all-round cricketer. Commuting, so to speak, between the Stock Exchange and Lord's, he rarely failed to make an impact for Middlesex whenever he turned out, either as batsman or fast bowler, or both.

The first of his 25 appearances for England was against Australia in the famous Lord's Test of 1930 when, substituting for Harold Larwood, he bowled expensively but, with A. P. F. Chapman, added 125 for the sixth wicket in the second innings. The following year he and L. E. G. Ames against New Zealand at Lord's combined in a stand of 246 which was for many years a world record for the eighth wicket in Tests, both making hundreds.

His choice for D. R. Jardine's MCC team to Australia in 1932–33 was strongly criticised. Yet he was one of the successes of the tour, taking 21 wickets in the Tests and averaging 23 with the bat. It is a matter of history that although entreated by his captain to do so he declined to bowl 'bodyline', and was always frank in his disapproval of it. Allen first led England in the 1936 series against

India, in obvious preparation for the captaincy in Australia the following winter. After winning the first two Tests there, England were defeated in the following three — thanks chiefly to some phenomenal scoring by Bradman.

In 1938 Allen was commissioned into the Territorial Army, and after serving in the City of London Yeomanry ('the Rough Riders') he joined an anti-aircraft battery which defended RAF Fighter Command HQ at Stanmore and Canvey Island. He was invited into Dowding's celebrated 'ops' room and developed a close relationship with the RAF which led to a posting as flak liaison officer at Bomber Command's No. 5 group. Determined to assess enemy anti-aircraft fire in action, Allen flew over the Ruhr in the air gunner's seat of a Handley Page Hampden in the autumn of 1940. His increasing flak expertise was then used, first as GSO2 of MI 14E and then as GSO1, in the rank of lieutenant colonel, with MI 15 (as the War Office centre for collating intelligence on German air defences became known). He was awarded the American Legion of Merit.

Just as Allen's leadership in Australia before the war had come in for the highest praise on all counts, so it did again in 1947-48 in the West Indies, even though he was now 45 and, with a weak side, MCC could not match the emergent brilliance of the 'three W's', Worrell, Weekes and Walcott. He was a model touring captain in that he took infinite trouble over every member of his side. At his best Allen was a valuable Test all-rounder, a fast bowler whose speed stemmed from a perfect action, a sound bat and excellent close fielder. Allen's most notable feat was in 1929 at Lord's when he took all 10 Lancashire wickets for 40 runs, this after arriving late on the field (by arrangement, naturally) and so missing the new ball. In county cricket at Lord's it was a unique feat, and so it remains.

The Lord's Committee Room was the scene of his work for cricket from 1932 to 1985 – an unprecedented span interrupted only by the Second World War. In 1963–64 he was president, and from 1964 to 1976 held the club's key post of treasurer. An amateur in the most complete sense on the field, Allen was very much a professional in committee. No one had a wider knowledge of every facet of cricket politics and administration. No one was better briefed, nor, it should be added, more tenacious in his opinions. He had more time than most, and he could show infinite patience in order to win his point. It was sometimes whispered that the easiest way to get a thing through was to persuade the *eminence grise* that it had been his own idea. There is no doubt he could be difficult. Likewise, it generally had to be admitted in the end that 'Gubby is probably right'.

Allen was the chief instigator of the national post-war movement in cricket for the involvement and teaching of the young. This was hitherto an uncharted field, but now there are associations covering every area. It led to Allen's authorship with H. S. Altham of *The MCC Coaching Book*, a best-seller for many generations.

When England and Australia were very much at odds over the perilous issue of throwing after the MCC tour of 1958–59 it was Allen who, with Sir Donald Bradman's eventual strong co-operation, devised a successful formula for eliminating the 'chucker'. He performed no more vital service than this.

Not the least of his labours was his seven seasons' chairmanship of the Test selectors from 1955 to 1961. Allen was not only a shrewd judge of a cricketer but he was also, on the testimony of all who served with him, an admirably fair and thorough chairman with a flair for finding the man for the occasion. In all he did there shone his great devotion to the game and a helpful, unfailing friendliness to all cricketers.

He was appointed CBE in 1962 and knighted in 1986. Gubby Allen never married. His family said he was always wedded to cricket.

A. P. F. CHAPMAN

Beat Australia six times running

Chapman, Arthur Percy Frank   Amateur

b: The Mount, Reading, Berkshire, 3 September 1900

Sch: Oakham and Uppingham   *Teams:* Cambridge U., Kent, MCC, England, Tennyson to Jamaica

Career batting:
394-554-44-16309-260-31.97; hundreds 27-*ct* 356
Bowling: 921-22-41.86

Test batting:
26-36-4-925-121-28.90; hundreds 1-*ct* 32
Bowling: 20-0

d: Alton, Hampshire, 16 September 1961. Aged 61.

A. P. F. Chapman was one of the most successful of all England Test captains. He was also, in the view of the more reliable judges among his contemporaries, one of the best. I stress the point early in this appreciation because the popular conception of Percy Chapman in his heyday was only partly true. He was debonair, generous, carefree in character as in his cricket, and as such the sporting world took him to its heart. Yet underlying the boyish facade was both a shrewd cricket brain and the good sense to ask advice from those of greater experience. With Jack Hobbs at his side Chapman had not far to look. He showed, too, a sympathy for people which naturally in its turn brought the very best out of them. His sides were happy sides.

Chapman's cricket was marked for distinction from his days at Uppingham at the end of the First War. As a schoolboy he played at Lord's with G. T. S. Stevens, D. R. Jardine, C. H. Gibson, L. P. Hedges, C. T. Ashton and N. E. Partridge: that was the best of all school vintages. His adventurous left-handed batting and fielding won him a Cambridge blue as a freshman. He was one of A. C. MacLaren's legendary side that beat the 1921 Australians at Eastbourne, and in 1922 made 102 not out in the University match, followed the next week by 160 in Gentlemen and Players. This latter innings against the cream of the professional bowling perhaps marked him out as a coming Test cricketer. Eight years later he completed an almost unique trilogy with 121 at Lord's against Australia. (M. P. Donnelly is the only other man to have scored centuries at Lord's in two classics and also in a Test match.)

Chapman played first for England in 1924 against South Africa and went that winter to Australia with A. E. R. Gilligan's side. Thereafter he was practically a permanent member of the England XI until the end of the MCC tour of South Africa in 1930–31. He led England in 17 Tests, of which nine were won and only two lost, including the Lord's Test already referred to against Australia. Prior to that he had won six successive Tests against them, an unrepeatable sequence.

Too venturesome to be a consistent scorer, he could turn a game by his hitting as quickly and as thoroughly as any cricketer of his generation or since. In 1927 at Mote Park after five Kent wickets had fallen for 70, he and G. B. Legge made 284 together in 2½ hours. Chapman made 260 in just over 3 hours, the last 50 in a quarter of an hour.

Not least he was a superb fielder, in the country in his undergraduate days, but for England and Kent close to the bat, mostly at gully and silly mid-off.

Hail-fellow-well-met with everyone, he became towards the end of his cricket career the victim of his popularity and from the war onwards his life went into sad eclipse. In the last few years his health grew so bad that he could not get to Lord's. The elderly and the middle-aged will recall him rather in his handsome sunlit youth, the epitome of all that was gay and fine in the game of cricket.

P. G. H. FENDER

The captain that never was

Fender, Percy George Herbert

Amateur

b: Balham, London, 22 August 1892

Sch: St George's, Weybridge and St Paul's

Teams: Sussex, Surrey, MCC, England, Tennyson to Jamaica

Career batting:
557-783-69-19034-185-26.65; hundreds 21-*ct* 600
Bowling: 47458-1894-25.05-100-16-8/24

Test batting:
13-21-1-380-60-19.00; *ct* 14
Bowling: 1185-29-40.86

d: Exeter, Devon, 15 June 1985. Aged 92.

Percy George Herbert Fender, the Surrey and England cricketer, was one of the best-known personalities of the inter-war years, a figure of glamour on the field and, occasionally, of mild controversy off it. As a St Paul's schoolboy he played first at 17 for Sussex in 1910, changing his allegiance in 1914 to Surrey and helping them not a little by his all-round cricket, to win the championship of that year, shortened as it was by the declaration of war. Afterwards his reputation quickly grew as an unorthodox, dangerous hitter, a guileful leg-break bowler, and a brilliant slip-catcher. In 1920 at Northampton he reached a hundred in 35 minutes – a time which to this day has not been bettered, though in a farcical travesty of the game it was equalled by Steven O'Shaughnessy in 1983 for Lancashire against Leicestershire. He went with J. W. H. T. Douglas's MCC side to Australia in 1920–21 and pulled his weight on a tour in which, so soon after the war, England laboured at a crippling disadvantage. He also toured

South Africa in 1922–23, and played 13 times in all for England, with a respectable degree of success.

His great deeds, however, were for Surrey, both as player and for a span of eleven summers (1921–31) as captain. To his leadership he brought much the same characteristics as he showed in his own cricket. In a more formal age he was an experimenter, always looking for a gamble and not infrequently bringing it off. Despite the perfection of the Oval wickets, and with generally slender bowling to discount great batting strength, he often came near to winning the Championship without ever quite doing so.

Often in the twenties he was tipped as captain of England, but other men were preferred, some scarcely his equal either as captains or cricketers. He was said not be in favour 'at Lord's' partly because of his outspokenness, and the fact of his periodic ventures into cricket journalism. He also wrote in the idiom of the day four books on Anglo–Australian Test series: reference works which have their value still. Spectacles, receding chin, silk neckerchief and unusually long sweaters made him the cartoonist's dream. With his tall, slim figure, dark, crinkly hair, horn-rimmed spectacles, no one, surely, of the older generation who saw him play will forget him.

At his best he was a highly effective as well as spectacular cricketer. Six times between 1921 and 1928 he did the double of a thousand runs and a hundred wickets. In 1923, when he made 1,427 runs and took 178 wickets, not even cricketers of such quality as Rhodes, Woolley, Roy Kilner or Tate had better all-round figures.

In the wake of the unreal BBC 'Bodyline' programmes it should be added that the portrayal of Fender was a caricature ridiculous to all who knew him.

A. E. R. GILLIGAN

Hail fellow well met

Gilligan, Arthur Edward Robert   Amateur

b: Denmark Hill, London, 23 December 1894

Sch: Dulwich   *Teams:* Cambridge U., Surrey, Sussex, MCC, England

Career batting:
337-510-55-9140-144-20.08; hundreds 12-*ct* 180
Bowling: 20141-868-23.20

Test batting:
11-16-3-209-39*-16.07; *ct* 3
Bowling: 1046-36-29.05

d: Mare Hill, Pulborough, Sussex, 5 September 1976. Aged 81.

Arthur Edward Robert Gilligan captained England in two Test series in the mid-twenties and had a close association with Sussex cricket lasting from the end of the First War until his death. Arthur Gilligan, like his brothers, F.W. and A.H.H., spent a lifetime in the game, his work when his playing days were over covering almost every field. His first administrative post was in 1926 when he was one of the selectors who chose the team which after three barren series won back the Ashes at The Oval.

On giving up the Sussex captaincy in 1930 he turned his hand for a while to cricket writing and broadcasting. But he was soon immersed again in the affairs of Sussex, and thereafter a large part of his life revolved around the ground at Hove. Yet he also played a conspicuous part in the world of golf, being in 1959 president of the English Golf Union. He was president also until his death of the County Cricketers' Golfing Society, having been chosen for both these offices no doubt because of his warmly 'clubbable' nature.

Gilligan was essentially a friendly man, hail-fellow-well-met, and it is hard to think that in the world of sport he ever made an enemy.

It must have been this characteristic which prompted the late Lord Harris (as it is commonly believed) to back him so strongly for the captaincy of MCC in Australia in 1924–25. Gilligan, however, was at his brief best a fast bowler of true England rank, whose great feat was, in company with Maurice Tate at Edgbaston in 1924, to bowl out South Africa for 30 on a good wicket (A.E.R.G., six for seven runs). At this moment the Sussex pair were the scourge of all-comers. A few weeks before this performance they had bowled out Surrey, at The Oval of all places, for 53, and Middlesex at Lord's for 104 and 41. The spell ended when Gilligan was hit over the heart when batting for the Gentlemen at The Oval. Next day, going in at No. 10, he made a dazzling 119 in an hour and a half. But the reaction to the blow was only delayed and it is generally agreed that he was never the same cricketer thereafter.

In Australia his bowling was rather expensive, but his leadership did much to restore English cricket to its old position of respect with the Australian public after the happenings of 1920 and 1921. After losing the third Test at Adelaide by 11 runs to cede the rubber England under Gilligan won the fourth Test at Melbourne by an innings to gain their first post-war victory. His record as an all-rounder is notable enough but off the field I judge his endeavours to have been of even greater value to cricket.

MOLLY HIDE

She symbolised women's cricket

Hide, Mary Edith   Amateur

b: Shanghai, 24 October 1913

Sch: Wycombe Abbey

Test batting:
15-27-3-872-124*-36.8
Bowling: 536-35-15.8

d: Godalming, Surrey, 10 October 1995. Aged 81.

When the Women's Cricket Association, founded at Colwall in 1926, began to spread its wings in the 1930s it was clearly in need of a figure who would be respected in the public mind as, one might say, the acceptable face of Women's Cricket. Molly Hide, handsome, dignified and an outstanding player, filled the picture to perfection.

One day on the Saffrons ground at Eastbourne she mentioned sadly to me how difficult it was for the press to take women's cricket seriously. Knowing how susceptible was Plum Warner, founder and editor of *The Cricketer*, to feminine charms, I invited her to meet him at Lord's over lunch (2/6 a head in the MCC dining room for him and me, 3/6 for her!). By the end of it the ladies had been promised a regular foothold in the magazine.

At The Oval in 1937 I saw Miss Hide lead her braves on to the field against Australia, agonised as poor Betty Snowball was run out for 99, and admired the cricket played by the talented and stylish triumvirate of Myrtle Maclagan, Snowball and Hide. Thereafter I could but follow and admire from afar, largely through the writings of her contemporary and close friend, Netta Rheinberg.

Molly Hide had gone on the first Women's tour to Australia and New Zealand as an undergraduate of Reading University aged 18, and made a hundred in the opening match. When she returned to Australia as captain in 1948–49 she topped the batting and bowling averages, and hit five hundreds, including one in a Test match. After her retirement following 17 years as England captain, like a good trouper she worked to put back into cricket something of the pleasure she had from it. Her knowledge and flair for the game and inspired leadership made her unique.

SIR LEONARD HUTTON

Ashes recovered and retained

Hutton, Sir Leonard   Professional

b: Fulneck, Pudsey, Yorkshire, 23 June 1916

Sch: Littlemoor Council School   *Teams:* Yorkshire, MCC, England

Career batting:
513-814-91-40140-364-55.51; hundreds 129-*ct* 400
Bowling: 5106-173-29.51

Test batting:
79-138-15-6971-364-56.67; hundreds 19-*ct* 57
Bowling: 232-3-77.33

d: Kingston-upon-Thames, Surrey, 6 September 1990. Aged 74.

Sir Leonard Hutton died at Kingston Hospital, Surrey, following an operation for a ruptured aorta, the main artery of the heart. Though the end came suddenly, he had been in frail health for some years. At the Oval Test a fortnight earlier his appearance saddened his friends. The quizzical smile peculiarly his own, as though he were enjoying some private joke – the expression by which many will remember him – emerged now and then, but keeping cheerful was plainly an effort. He was an essentially quiet, reticent man, though capable of sudden shafts of humour. From his earliest days with Yorkshire there was a natural dignity about him which remained through life. Through the most stressful moments he appeared outwardly unruffled. The good name of cricket meant much to him, and he was only caustic about those who sullied it.

Sir Leonard Hutton holds a secure place among the household names of cricket. He will be remembered as in lineal descent from the great players who, before him, wore the white rose of Yorkshire, as the holder of the record score of 364 in Tests between

England and Australia, and as the captain who recovered the Ashes in 1953 and retained them 'down under' 18 months later. The strain of leadership on a sensitive, introverted personality, coupled with the responsibility of continuing to open the England innings, led shortly after these successes to what was then considered a premature retirement six months short of his 40th birthday. The award of a knighthood closely followed, the second, and to date the last, bestowed upon an English professional cricketer. His predecessor was Sir Jack Hobbs, still remembered as 'The Master', whose last days with Surrey in the early summer of 1934 coincided exactly with Hutton's first with Yorkshire. Hutton, like his great forerunner, was far from robust in physique. Each had reached the peak of his skill when war interrupted his cricket, in Hobbs's case for four years, in Hutton's for six. The course that their careers subsequently took reflects the respective demands made upon them. After the First War Hobbs made only three tours, all to Australia, before his retirement 15 years later at the age of 51. In the decade after the Second War Hutton's shoulders were burdened with 16 series, at home and abroad. He toured Australia three times, the West Indies twice and South Africa for a second time during this period. In all but his last tour he was the mainstay of England's batting. In the Australian series of 1950–51 and 1953 his average was virtually double that of anyone on either side.

If Hobbs be acknowledged as the greatest of all professional batsmen, Len Hutton by common consent must rate pre-eminently with two others of equal pedigree, Denis Compton and Walter Hammond. These two were more flamboyant in style than he, as befitted their place at number four in the order. There was more self-denial about Hutton's opening role, a characteristic inherited in full from his mentor and partner, Herbert Sutcliffe. But he too could dazzle when he deemed the time was right.

Leonard Hutton was born a mile from the celebrated cricket nursery of Pudsey in the adjacent village of Fulneck. Several generations of Huttons had belonged to the self-sufficient community which the mid-European Moravian sect had established there in the 19th century. His father and grandfather were builders. Naturally the village had its cricket ground, where the minister bowled to him as well as his father, uncles and brothers. All were dedicated cricketers. Moving on to Pudsey St Lawrence, Len was only 13 when he was bidden to the Yorkshire nets at Headingley. Len never forgot what George Hirst said after he had first seen him bat. 'Well played. Try and improve on that.' Another great Yorkshire cricketer, Sutcliffe, was much more effusive in his comment, so much so that the question was whether Len had been burdened with prophesies too extravagant for a youngster's good. However, this one always kept a clear head on his shoulders.

He recovered from a duck in his first innings for Yorkshire shortly before his 18th birthday, and from another (his scores 0 and 1) on his debut for England a few days after his 21st. There had never been doubt about his method, while as his career unfolded his temperament proved equally reliable. He made the first of his 19 Test hundreds in his second match, against New Zealand, while both he and Compton scored hundreds in their first Tests against Australia at Trent Bridge the following summer. In the fifth Test, in August 1938, the first and the last 'timeless' Test to be played in England, he produced the ultimate marathon of endurance, an innings of 364 which was both the highest Test score and at 13 hours 20 minutes the longest ever played.

As a boy young Len had seen the making of the score he had now surpassed, the 334 at Headingley by Don Bradman, who was thereupon installed as his hero. The first of his seven MCC tours followed, to South Africa. In 1939 he made 12 hundreds, two for England v West Indies, ten for Yorkshire. When war came, Hutton was at the top of the tree, a well-nigh ideal model for imitation. Perfect positioning of the feet and faultless balance at the moment of impact gave him the timing that a modest physique demanded. These attributes became the more important when in 1941 he suffered a serious gymnasium accident, falling on his left arm during Commando training. This resulted in several operations, the arm in question emerging from 14 months in plaster emaciated and three inches shorter than the right. The lengthy recuperation period naturally involved also an adjustment of his batting technique.

Hutton was at the centre of the picture in all England's postwar Test series, along with Compton, and notably in the duels against the Australian fast bowling pair of Lindwall and Miller. In 1952, as the most seasoned and level-headed among the leading professionals, he was promoted to the captaincy of England, the first of his kind since the early missionary tours to Australia in the 1870s. He wore the mantle of leadership with unruffled dignity if little indication of comfort. India were disposed of easily in England in 1952 in preparation for the Australian visit following. After four fluctuating draws Hutton, himself playing the highest innings of the match, brought the Ashes back home at The Oval after a record absence of 19 years. So far, so very good. In that 1953–54 winter was due another visit to the West Indies, against whom England had already lost two post-war rubbers. Dubious though many were at the prospect of his handling all the problems of a tour to fervent and politically emerging countries, MCC made the cardinal error of departing from established custom, appointing not an experienced tour manager but a player-manager in C.H. Palmer, a younger member of the team who had not hitherto played for England. Wholesale defeats in the first two Tests saw English prestige at its lowest, both on the playing field and off it.

The subsequent recovery, to the point of halving the series, owed most to the captain who, draining himself to the furthest point of nervous and physical exhaustion, played successive innings of 169, 44, 30 not out and 205. If it was not a happy tour, much was redeemed by its ending.

In the following English summer, when Pakistan were the visitors prior to the forthcoming MCC tour of Australia and New Zealand, Hutton's hold on the captaincy did not go unquestioned. In his absence because of 'acute neuritis due to overstrain' the selectors, despite the fact that he was at a theological college, turned to D. S. Sheppard (later Bishop of Liverpool), a batsman of clear leadership credentials although soon to be lost to the game. The implications of this move caused a rare clamour and a Press outcry lasting until Hutton's reappointment late in July.

Up to a point England's fortunes in Australia followed the West Indies course in that the first Test ended in wholesale defeat. Now, however, two young amateur batsmen, Peter May and Colin Cowdrey, saved their side in successive Tests while Frank Tyson emerged as a match-winning fast bowler. A narrow victory in the second Test was followed by two by wider margins, the second of which secured the retention of the Ashes. Hutton had handled his side with quiet, shrewd assurance, though it has to be said that the tactic of slowing down the over rate dates from this tour.

The captain returned home to a hero's welcome. He was appointed captain for all five Tests against South Africa, an unprecedented mark of confidence, and by passing a new rule MCC were able to make him an Honorary Cricket Member while still a player. But in personal terms the cost of Len's three-year span had now to be accepted. His batting in the Australian Tests had been an unaccustomed struggle, and in the MCC–South African match in May he was stricken with lumbago and forced to withdraw, as he did soon afterwards from the England captaincy. He managed ten matches for Yorkshire, in between aches and pains, and in the penultimate one came his 129th – and last – hundred, against Notts at Trent Bridge.

After reaching a characteristically flawless unhurried hundred in about three and a half hours he suddenly blossomed into a stream of the most brilliant strokes, so that his last 94 runs actually came in 65 minutes. As at Sydney and Brisbane, for instance, in Test matches, the Roundhead had revealed a Cavalier struggling to burst forth. Hutton needs no figures to illustrate his mastery as a batsman. Confined to 16 home seasons and seven in the sun and heat of tours, his tally of 40,140 tells its own story. In Tests his 6,971 runs were made at an average of 56. Given a full career without intermission or accident, who can tell what his record might have been?

After retirement he covered Test matches for the *Observer* newspaper and served as a Test selector in 1975–77. A former president of the Forty Club, he had recently accepted the presidency of Yorkshire.

BRIAN SELLERS

Lord Hawke's successor

Sellers, Arthur Brian, MBE   Amateur

b: Keighley, Yorkshire, 5 March 1907

Sch: St. Peter's, York   *Team:* Yorkshire

Career batting:
344-455-53-9270-204-23.05; hundreds 4-*ct* 273
Bowling: 676-9-75.11

d: Eldwick, Bingley, Yorkshire, 20 February 1981. Aged 73.

Arthur Brian Sellers was second among Yorkshire captains only to Lord Hawke alike in the length of his reign and the number of championships won. In his nine seasons, starting in 1933 and ending in 1947, Yorkshire won the title six times. He was second perhaps to his most famous predecessor in another sphere also, for as chairman of the cricket committee after his retirement until his resignation in 1972 he also wielded wide authority within the club, though never to the extent of Lord Hawke, who had been Yorkshire's benevolent dictator for nearly half a century.

Sellers rendered his most valuable services to Yorkshire on the field of play, coming in almost untried and succeeding by sheer determination and force of character in getting the best out of a side most of whom were his seniors in age as all were in repute. His methods were direct, to say the least, but his men 'took it' because they recognised his essential fairness and his overriding pride in Yorkshire cricket. Moreover he was at least the equal of any of them (except Arthur Mitchell) as a fielder and in insisting on the highest standards in this respect he certainly led by example. Yorkshire's batting was so strong that they were seldom short of runs. But he improved to the extent of making himself a valuable man at a pinch, as may be seen from his career average of 23 for a total of 9,270. Thrice he made 1,000 runs in a season, and of his four hundreds one was against the Australians, another against the fast Notts attack of Larwood and Voce. Allowing the quality at his command, it could be claimed for him in the late thirties that there was no better captain in England.

He was a selector off and on from 1938 to 1955, and helped pick the MCC team to Australia in 1946, before joining the Press party as a journalist. Late in the tour he voiced forthright criticism of Walter Hammond's captaincy which, justified though it may have been, was thought not to come well from one of those who had appointed him. Sellers was widely blamed, but unluckily so in that what developed into an angry controversy began with remarks made in private and not intended for publication.

His playing days finished, he brought his bluff outspokenness to a post-war generation of cricketers to whom his manner was less acceptable than to their forerunners, and in the troubles between the county and several of their most famous players Sellers was at the centre of the storm. When an action group within the club sought to bring down the committee in 1971 – and in fact defeated them at a meeting attended by more than a thousand members – after the sacking of Brian Close in favour of Geoffrey Boycott, their chief target was Brian Sellers. He was in some ways a paradoxical character, a strange blend of modesty and over-confidence. Tact was never his strong suit, but whatever his ups and downs, no one ever questioned either his courage or his single-minded devotion to Yorkshire cricket.

WILF WOOLER

'He hardly suffered fools at all, let alone gladly'

Wooller, Wilfred   Amateur

b: Rhos-on-Sea, Denbighshire, 20 November 1912

Sch: Rydal   *Teams:* Cambridge U., Glamorgan

Career batting:
430-679-77-13593-128-22.57; hundreds 5-*ct* 413
Bowling: 25830-958-26.96

d: 10 March 1997. Aged 84.

Wilfred Wooller was a games player of astonishing versatility: a renowned Welsh rugby international; captain of the Glamorgan side that won the county cricket championship in 1948; a soccer player good enough to play (albeit once) for Cardiff City; a squash player for Wales; an outstanding sprinter and long-jumper; and an accomplished performer at water polo.

At rugby football Wilf Wooller was one of the greatest centre three-quarters of all time. The *Daily Telegraph*'s Howard Marshall wrote of 'his tremendous pace and his siege-gun kicking, and his ability to win a game on his own by some gargantuan thrust. Wooller was tall and strongly built (even as a schoolboy he weighed 13 stone), and when he was in full flight for the line seemed to eat up the earth as if he were covering it with seven league boots.'

Particularly memorable was his performance for Wales against the All Blacks in December 1935. The All Blacks were in the lead when, just after half-time, Wooller received the ball in his own half, at full stride. 'And what a stride it was,' Howard Marshall reported. 'A strange loping stride, with those long legs going like pistons, carrying him bang through the shallow defence, while 50,000 screamed. "He's away – he's away!" they shouted – 10, 20, 30 yards – the powerful Gilbert coming in to tackle – Wooller punting over his head, racing after the bouncing ball, over-running it on the line, and there was Rees-Jones dashing in from the wing to touch down for a most glorious try.' Three minutes from time Wooller and Rees-Jones combined in much the same manner to score another try, and Wales had won a famous victory by 13 points to 12. In celebration, Wooller required little assistance in heaving a piano over the banisters of the team's hotel into the foyer below. He would play for Wales 18 times and captained the side in 1938–39.

As a cricketer Wooller was one of the last true amateurs, a fast-medium bowler, robust hitter and intrepid close fielder. But it was as captain that he excelled. He first led the Glamorgan side in 1947 and the next year inspired them to wholly unexpected triumph in the county championship. Nine of the team had been born in Wales, and the spirit that Wooller engendered – expressed in aggressive fielding and brilliant catching around the bat (with the captain to the fore at short leg) – carried off the championship. 'It was two seasons before Jim Swanton would believe it,' he recalled with relish.

Wilfred Wooller was the son of a builder. He was educated at Rydal School, and won his first cap for Wales at the age of 20 in 1933. Later that year he went up to Christ's College, Cambridge, where he became a double blue for rugby and cricket.

During his three years in the Cambridge XV he formed a remarkable partnership with the fly-half Cliff Jones. In his first Varsity match, 1933, Cambridge lost 3–5, but the next year they scored a crushing 29–4 victory against an Oxford side which con-tained eight then or future internationals. In that game Wooller scored a gigantic drop goal from within his own half; as he recalled it, the ball (of heavy leather, not the modern plastic) landed in Twickenham's north stand.

Wooller went on to play for Sale and Cardiff. In the summer he won a place in the Glamorgan side under Maurice Turnbull, another great Welsh games-player of Cambridge pedigree. In 1939 he made 111 and took six wickets as Glamorgan defeated the West Indies by 73 runs. At the outbreak of the Second World War Wooller was commissioned into the Royal Artillery. Captured by the Japanese in Java in 1942 he spent the rest of the war in a PoW camp. Though he was not submitted to the worst excesses of the Japanese, imprisonment was a trial to someone of his personality: he hardly suffered fools at all, let alone gladly. His years at Glamorgan (he retired as a player in 1960 but continued as secretary until 1977) were peppered with controversy; on one occasion he provoked the resignation of half the committee.

Wooller's views were right-wing and authoritarian. He had been brought up, he said, 'as a God-fearing man with a respect for the Establishment'. He held that 'leadership qualities improve with the right training. Often that came from the right schooling.' He was never averse to a row. When the South African rugger team toured Britain in 1969–70 and was subjected to protests from the anti-apartheid lobby, Wooller told the Archbishop of Wales that support for the demonstrators was 'disgraceful', an example of the 'usual un-Christian attitude' to be found in the Church. Ninety-nine per cent of the trouble, he suggested, was caused by 'Lefties, weirdies and odd bods'.

He described Denis Howell, Labour's sports minister, as 'not unlike a 50p piece – double-faced, many-sided and not worth a great deal'. Howell's successor, the Conservative Eldon Griffiths, was dismissed as a politician playing at sport. Wooller was a Test selector from 1955 to 1961, and in 1961 served on Col. R. S. Rait Kerr's committee on the future of cricket. From 1961 to 1988 he wrote about rugby and cricket for the *Sunday Telegraph*. His views were trenchant, and he did not warm to the training methods and technical dedication of modern players.

Wooller married first, in 1941 (dissolved 1947), Lady Gillian Windsor-Clive, eldest daughter of the 2nd Earl of Plymouth. He married secondly, in 1948, Enid James; they had three sons and two daughters.

R. E. S. WYATT

Lived to be a patriarch

Wyatt, Robert Elliott Storey   Amateur

b: Milford, Surrey, 2 May 1901

Sch: King Henry VIII, Coventry   *Teams:* Warwickshire,
Worcestershire, MCC, England

Career batting:
739-1141-157-39405-232-40.04; hundreds 85-*ct* 415- *st* 1
Bowling: 29597-901-32.84

Test batting:
40-64-6-1839-149-31.70; hundreds 2-*ct* 16
Bowling: 642-18-35.66

d: 20 April 1995. Aged 93.

R. E. S. Wyatt was England's senior Test captain for many years, a patriarch whose achievement over a playing career lasting nearly 30 years has been bettered only by a handful. Wyatt's appointment to lead England in the Ashes-deciding fifth Test against Australia at the Oval in 1930 – in place of the popular and successful A. P. F. Chapman – was a sensation comparable in those days only to the dropping of A. W. Carr in favour of Chapman against Australia four years earlier.

Chapman's promotion had brought success. Wyatt's did not – though small blame attached to him. He led England, soundly if without inspiration, 15 times in his 40 Test appearances, including the 1934 home series against Australia, MCC's tour of the West Indies in 1934–35 and South Africa's visit to England in 1935. Wyatt was vice-captain to D. R. Jardine in Australia in 1932–3 and to G. O. Allen there in 1936–7, fulfilling both roles to general satisfaction. The first was especially taxing, in that he strongly opposed the bodyline tactics.

Bob Wyatt was a scion of the architectural dynasty and a cousin of the future Lord Wyatt of Weeford; he was educated at King Henry VIII School, Coventry. He played for Warwickshire from 1923, with little impact at first. But he persevered, improving gradually until a successful MCC tour to India in 1926–27 promised greater things. The next winter he toured South Africa with MCC and, after beginning his Test career with a duck, held his England place in a drawn series.

Against South Africa at Old Trafford in 1929 Wyatt made the first post-war Test hundred by an amateur, and over the next decade established himself as one of the most dependable batsmen in England, with periodic effectiveness as a medium-pace change bowler. Between 1927–28 and 1936–37 he played in 13 Test series, succeeding Jardine as captain on the latter's retirement in 1934. Though England were thwarted in 1934 by the brilliance of Bradman and the spin partnership of O'Reilly and Grimmett, Wyatt had the satisfaction (thanks to a thunderstorm and Hedley Verity's bowling) of leading England to what remains the only victory over Australia at Lord's since 1896.

Wyatt took over the Warwickshire captaincy in 1930 and held it for eight years, at the end of which the committee – seeking a more zestful approach – announced the appointment of Peter Cranmer, the 23-year-old captain of England at rugby football. The matter was not handled tactfully; though Wyatt continued to play under Cranmer for the two remaining pre-war summers, he was deeply hurt.

After the war he moved across the border to Worcestershire, where he had six happy summers, latterly as captain. In those three years under his leadership their Championship places were 3rd, 6th and 4th. It was the most successful phase in the county's history to that point. At Taunton in 1951, in the last week of his last season (and now past 50), he faced the last ball of the match against Somerset with six runs needed to win: he duly drove it high into the pavilion for victory. Almost 20 years earlier he and C. F. Walters had made 160 together at Lord's in an opening partnership of an hour and a half, which brought the Gentlemen, under his leadership, to their first victory over the Players since the First World War.

Bob Wyatt was all of a piece, bulldog in looks and spirit, his cricket a perfect reflection of the man. In mid-March 1935, in the Jamaica Test match, a fast ball from Martindale lifted and fractured his jaw in four places with a noise like a rifle shot. When he recovered consciousness Bob called for pen and paper and wrote that he attached no blame to the bowler. Before being wheeled off to hospital he also revised the batting order. Six weeks later, leading MCC against Surrey at Lord's, he put himself in first and made a hundred. The next month he faced the fast South African attack at Trent Bridge and made 149, his highest score in Test cricket.

Bob was a selector from 1949 to 1953, and in Coronation Year helped to choose the team which recovered the Ashes – which he had had to surrender in 1934. He wrote an instructional book on the game, *The Ins and Outs of Cricket*, and a candid biography, *Three Straight Sticks*. He was a man of firm opinions, based on the closest study of the game. When the lbw law was broadened in 1936 he was almost alone in deploring it as detrimental to off-side play – a view since endorsed by history. Bob was deeply appreciative of two most rare distinctions accorded him in his closing years: the Life Vice-Presidency of MCC and the Freemanship of I Zingari.

In recent years Bob's determination enabled him to shake off a succession of strokes. Long resident in Cornwall, he was nevertheless regularly at Lord's in his tenth decade, with his devoted wife Mollie, as a resident guest in Paul Getty's box.

NORMAN YARDLEY
Captain in sunshine and shadow

Yardley, Norman Walter Dransfield   Amateur

b: Gawber, Barnsley, Yorkshire, 19 March 1915

Sch: St Peter's, York   *Teams:* Cambridge U., Yorkshire, MCC,
England, Tennyson to India

Career batting:
446-658-75-18173-183*-31.17; hundreds 27-*ct* 328-*st* 1
Bowling: 8506-279-30.48

Test batting:
20-34-2-812-99-25.37; *ct* 14
Bowling: 707-21-33.66

d: Lodge Moor, Sheffield, Yorkshire, 3 October 1989. Aged 74.

Norman Yardley was a household name in the early post-war years, captain first of England in 1947 and then of Yorkshire. He led England to victory over South Africa in 1947, and Yorkshire to the county championship (shared with Middlesex) in 1949 in the second of his eight summers as their captain. After two years as chairman of the Test selectors, in 1951 and 1952, he later turned to journalism and broadcasting, where his equable and generous nature was reflected in reasoned, charitable comment.

At St Peter's School, York, Yardley distinguished himself as a squash player (winning the Drysdale Cup two years running) as well as a cricketer. A true all-rounder, at Cambridge he won blues at cricket, squash, hockey and rugby fives; he was six times North of England squash champion.

During the 1939–45 war he served with the Green Howards and was severely wounded in the Western Desert. Afterwards he toured Australia, becoming the first England cricketer to score 50 runs in each innings of a Test match and to take five wickets in the same game – at Melbourne in 1947.

Yardley was a sound bat of polished method, with a strong penchant for the on-side. He toured first with MCC to South Africa in 1938–39, and in 1946–47 fulfilled a much-needed function as vice-captain to W. R. Hammond in Australia. He averaged 31 with the bat and surprised himself most of all by taking Bradman's wicket three times running in the Tests with deceptively simple-looking medium pace. He made his highest Test score of 99 when in 1947 at Trent Bridge he and Denis Compton saved the game against South Africa after England had followed on.

Captain again in 1948, he could not prevent Bradman's powerful side from winning four of the five Tests, though twice England had a winning chance, in the first case at Old Trafford being in all probability deprived by the weather. Again he headed the bowling averages. He led England also in 1950 against the West Indies but was replaced by F. R. Brown when the selectors knew he could not make himself available once again for Australia. After Yorkshire's success in 1949 they were under him four times runners-up in the championship.

His last role in cricket was as president of Yorkshire, a hot seat bearing no relation to the sinecure of Lord Hawke's day. There was some truth in the criticism that Yardley governed an over-zealous bunch of tykes with too light a touch. He was indeed far removed from the popular idea of a Yorkshire cricketer, being a man of tact and charm who never made an enemy.

8

ALL-ROUNDERS

LES AMES

'All that is most admirable . . .'

Ames, Leslie Ethelbert George, CBE   Professional

b: Elham, Kent, 3 December 1905

Sch: Harvey GS, Folkestone   *Teams:* Kent, MCC, England,
                                   Commonwealth

Career batting:
593-951-95-37248-295-43.51; hundreds 102-*ct* 704 *st* 417
Bowling: 801-24-33.37

Test batting:
47-72-12-2434-149-40.56; hundreds 8-*ct* 74 *st* 23

d: Canterbury, Kent, 22 February 1990. Aged 84.

Les Ames, the Kent and England cricketer, epitomised all that is most admirable in the world of games. After a distinguished playing career, during which he kept wicket in 47 Tests, Ames became the first professional to be appointed a selector, a role he filled to general approval for eight years. It was one of a number of firsts for a 'pro'. In the 1960s he managed three MCC sides abroad, including the 1967–68 tour to the West Indies, the only series from which England returned victorious. When he relinquished the secretary-managership of Kent in 1975 after 18 years, he was nominated as President. He was also the first professional to be elected to the MCC Committee.

Leslie Ethelbert George Ames was born in 1905, into a cricketing family in the village of Elham, a few miles south of Canterbury. Blessed with a strong physique, young Les speedily rewarded the interest of two men who in his youth offered him particularly warm encouragement. One was F. A. MacKinnon, later Chief of his Clan, who had played for Kent in the dark ages, and in 1878 had accompanied Lord Harris's team to Australia. The

MacKinnon, who lived close by, gave Ames his first bat at the age of four and followed his career closely thereafter. G. J. V. Weigall was county coach when he spotted Ames shortly after he left Harvey Grammar School, Folkestone. Telling the promising young batsman that he must become 'double-barrelled' (an all-rounder) if he wanted to make cricket his career, Weigall ordered him to keep wicket. After a due apprenticeship on the Kent staff, Ames became the regular county wicket-keeper in 1927. His first hundred for the county earned him a silver claymore from the MacKinnon. Two years later he won the first of his England caps. The Second World War brought an end to his Test career, and his double activity as wicket-keeper and batsman. He joined the RAF in 1940, and rose to the rank of Squadron Leader.

In 1946 a youngster called Godfrey Evans succeeded him behind the stumps. But Ames was batting as well as ever when in 1950, aged 44, he scored his 100th first-class hundred, aptly enough to win a match against the clock in Canterbury Week. Then, in the first match of 1951, he 'went' so severely in the back that he was obliged to give up playing. Ames's unexpected retirement frustrated the intention of the Kent committee to make him their first professional captain.

If this catalogue of 'firsts' suggests perhaps a sycophantic or at least an acquiescent nature, the facts are otherwise. Les was never other than a plain speaker, conspicuously frank and utterly fair. He had no prejudices and was a sound judge of men. Hence his success in his selectorial and managerial roles. Les's philosophy derived no doubt from a happy boyhood, and from those early formative years in a Kent side rich in character, and with an approach to the game which at this distance seems almost impossibly idealistic. The senior professional over his first 12 summers was Frank Woolley, the most glamorous county cricketer of any generation – what a model for a naturally enterprising young batsman!

'Tich' Freeman, the great leg-spin and googly bowler, was at his peak when Ames began an association with him that is probably the most fruitful in history between wicket-keeper and bowler. Of his successive captains – Cornwallis, Evans, Legge, Chapman, Valentine and Chalk – Ames wrote with admiration and affection. Kent, with their professional-amateur mix, were indeed an attractive side, in which Ames's own performance was a main feature. When he made the first of his six MCC tours, with Chapman to Australia in 1928–29, as the youngest member of the side, it was as understudy to George Duckworth. He owed his first Test caps to his superiority as a batsman. But by the next Australian visit – the Bodyline tour of 1932–33 – Ames was recognised as a master of his craft, equally at home with speed and spin. Of all the wicket-keeper batsmen, none has bettered his Test average of 40 with eight hundreds. The first of these hundreds, against New Zealand at Lord's in 1931, involved him in a stand of 246 with G. O. B. Allen for the 8th wicket which is still a Test record in England. Three years later, in an innings of 120 against Australia, also at Lord's, he pulled England out of a hole in company with Maurice Leyland (109).

His achievement of thrice capturing more than a hundred victims, in addition to his habitual thousand runs, must be secure against time. J. T. Murray once got there; no one else. Even more certainly no one will ever match his 64 stumpings in 1932. The next year he made 3,000 runs (average 58), but had only 69 victims, handing over the gloves at times to another Kent keeper, due the following winter to win a Test cap, W.H.V. (Hopper) Levett.

Ames's batting was characterised by nimble footwork and a marked facility of timing, the two being generally complementary, and he loved going down the pitch to the spinners. Against fast bowling he was a compulsive hooker, and thus to some extent vulnerable. He is the only man to have twice won the Lawrence Trophy for the fastest hundred of the season. Both were made in less than 70 minutes.

In the last phase of his service for Kent, beginning in 1957, he took on the managership of the club at a low point in the county's history, and saw their fortunes change so much for the better that, under the leadership of Colin Cowdrey, the Championship was won in their centenary year, 1970. At the beginning of July in that summer Kent stood 17th in the table, at which point Ames addressed the team in forthright terms still recalled with awe by all who were present. After this they never looked back, and throughout the 1970s Kent went from strength to strength.

While by no means a diehard, Les held firmly to traditional sporting values. He deplored intimidation by fast bowlers, just as in his young days, keeping wicket to Larwood and Voce in 1932–33, he strongly deprecated Bodyline. He resolutely favoured uncovered pitches and was contemptuous of the pernicious habit of talking abusively to the batsmen – unknown in his day, and now euphemistically called 'sledging'. He always thought that both umpires and players were absurdly fussy about the light.

In his youth he played professional football for Clapton (now Leyton) Orient and Gillingham. In later years he was a hard man to beat on the golf course, and in his eighties he twice went round the Royal Cinque Ports in under his age. Les was then still regularly stepping out the eight miles or so from his Canterbury home to Elham, where so many years ago it used to be said that the boy hit your bowling all over the place, and you were then either bowled out by his father or given out by his umpiring grandfather. Except on duty for his county or his country he never strayed far from his roots.

F. R. BROWN

High marks as captain, not as manager

Brown, Frederick Richard, MBE   Amateur

b: Lima, Peru, 16 December 1910

Sch: The Leys   *Teams:* Cambridge U., Surrey,
                             Northamptonshire, MCC, England

Career batting:
335-536-49-13325-212-27.36; hundreds 22-*ct* 212
Bowling: 32007-1221-26.21

Test batting:
22-30-1-734-79-25.31; *ct* 22
Bowling: 1398-45-31.06

d: Ramsbury, Wiltshire, 24 July 1991. Aged 80.

The death of Frederick Richard Brown, the old England captain, removes a man whose life in cricket touched many points and lasted to the end. He played first for England as a Cambridge undergraduate in 1931 and finally, when 42, in 1953. He was then successively chairman of selectors, touring manager, president of MCC and chairman of both the Cricket Council and the National Cricket Association. He was president of the NCA until 1990.

Freddie Brown, large and strong, emerged from the Leys School as a dangerous wrist spinner and formidable attacking bat. Like other such contemporary Test cricketers as K. S. Duleepsinhji, I. A. R. Peebles, E. T. Killick and D. V. P. Wright, he owed much to the coaching of the great South African all-rounder, Aubrey Faulkner, at his first ever indoor school. At 20, he was making his mark for the University, Surrey and England. And the following year he went with MCC to Australia under D. R. Jardine.

His brand of cricket in no way fitted into his captain's scheme of things, and in the remaining pre-war years he merely gave periodic reminders of his skill as one of the many gifted amateurs who moved to and from club and county cricket – to the obvious advantage of both.

Captured at Tobruk in the Second World War, the loss of four and a half stone as a prisoner of war, and the subsequent necessity to earn a living, quenched Brown's further cricket ambitions until, in 1949, a business post came along which carried with it the prospect of reviving the gloomy fortunes of Northamptonshire. His career then entered a second phase. At Northampton, his robust leadership not only transformed that struggling side but brought him back into the limelight on the Test scene. In 1950, a tremendous innings at Lord's in the Gentlemen and Players match (122 out of 131 in less than two hours) won him the captaincy of England both at home against West Indies and of MCC in Australia and New Zealand.

On his return to Australia at a remove of 18 years, Brown's stout-hearted reaction to adversity was proof against the shortcomings of a weak side which was virtually carried by the combined efforts of Hutton, Bedser, Bailey and the captain. After losing the rubber, England won their first post-war victory over Australia at Melbourne (R.T. Simpson's admirable 156 not out was the innings of his life). To the Australians, with his bluff manner and friendly grin, Brown came across as the type of Englishman they most admired. Now 40, the captain led England successfully the following summer in a hard-fought rubber against South Africa. Nor was his Test cricket yet quite over, for, in 1953, when chairman of selectors, he was persuaded back at no small risk to his reputation against Australia at Lord's to fill the all-round gap. In an epic match, chiefly memorable for the saving stand between Watson and Bailey, he bowled 52 overs, took four wickets and made 50 runs.

There followed two MCC managerships abroad, in South Africa and Australia, which, frankly, did not altogether suit his style. Still to come, though, was a period of valuable service as an administrator.

J. G. W. DAVIES
Guardian of Cambridge cricket

Davies, Jack Gale Wilmot, OBE   Amateur

b: Broad Clyst, Devon, 10 September 1911

Sch: Tonbridge   *Teams:* Cambridge U., Kent, MCC

Career batting:
153-262-12-5982-168-23.92; hundreds 4-*ct* 87
Bowling: 7847-258-30.41

d: Cambridge, 5 November 1992. Aged 81.

Jack Davies was a sportsman of diverse gifts and an ample talent lightly worn. On the cricket field he radiated a contagious sense of enjoyment and humour. He was a dashing type of batsman, an off-spinner who had his days of glory, and a brilliant cover fielder whose casual air, shirt sleeves flapping, was a trap for the unwary. It is always remembered that at Cambridge on the first morning of the Australian match of 1934 he bowled Bradman for a duck with a straight one, the great man having played for a shade of turn. It was as though someone had committed an indiscretion in a cathedral. The perpetrator looked embarrassed: the treasurer of the CUCC and the growing Fenner's crowd were far from pleased. A week earlier, with a swift pounce and throw, he had sent back – also for a duck and in his first innings for Yorkshire – another cricketer due for fame, Len Hutton.

In the University match of 1934 Davies bowed out of undergraduate life by taking five for 43 against Oxford. He was the seventh bowler tried, with more than 300 on the board and only three wickets down. He tended to need an occasion to bring out his best; so his first-class figures scarcely reflect his true value. In an early match for Kent he snatched victory in a tough situation, taking seven Essex wickets for 20 in about an hour. He was always welcome in the side when available, continuing to play for the county until the age of 40. He went on playing club cricket, in particular for the Yellowhammers and the Buccaneers, for another twenty years.

From his retirement in 1951 he served almost until his death as resident overseer of Cambridge cricket. At Lord's in his later years he was of great value – first as Treasurer of MCC at the time of the Packer crisis, then in 1985–86 as President of MCC and so Chairman of the International Cricket Council. In the tackling of the game's many problems no one's view was accorded greater respect. He was finally made a life vice-president of MCC.

As a rugby footballer he could find no place among the gifted Cambridge backs of his day, but on coming down captained Blackheath as a centre three-quarter, played for Kent and got as far as an England trial. He was three times amateur champion at Rugby fives.

GODFREY EVANS
'A veritable jack-in-the-box'

Evans, Thomas Godfrey, CBE   Professional

b: Finchley, London, 18 August 1920

Sch: Kent College, Canterbury   *Teams:* Kent, MCC, England

Career batting:
465-753-52-14882-144-21.22; hundreds 7-*ct* 816-*st* 250

Test batting:
91-133-14-2439-104-20.49; hundreds 2-*ct* 173-*st* 46

d: Northampton, 3 May 1999. Aged 78.

Godfrey Evans, England's great wicket-keeper of the immediate post-war years was a boundlessly energetic, fast-moving,
quick-witted, ever-optimistic fellow and these characteristics were
perfectly reflected in his cricket. He conveyed through the longest
day a sense of enjoyment which made him a highly popular
figure with crowds everywhere. He was short, stocky and
immensely strong, a veritable jack-in-the-box.

Evans belonged to the generation which were just pushing their
way into first-class cricket when the War came. In Kent's last fixture of 1939 *Wisden* noted that Evans 'kept wicket specially well
on the first day'. He only did so because W. H. V. Levett, the regular keeper, had been called to the colours.

Evans was just 26 when in the third Test against India at The
Oval in 1946, after three months' first-class experience, he made
the first of his 91 almost consecutive appearances for England. For
the next 13 years he reigned supreme behind the stumps, making
four tours with MCC to Australia, and two each to South Africa
and the West Indies.

Half-way through the summer of 1959 (following England's
total eclipse in Australia the previous winter) the selectors passed
him over 'in the interests of team-building'. Godfrey was not one

to lag superfluous. Expected to make runs batting for England at number 7, his work-load had been almost heavier than that of any of his contemporaries, Accordingly, aged 39, he promptly announced his retirement. Essentially a man for the big occasion, he left at the top.

Thomas Godfrey Evans was born on 18 August 1920 at Finchley, north London, but was brought up in Kent and won his colours and became captain of cricket, football and hockey at Kent College, Canterbury. His early sporting instincts were divided between cricket and boxing. He won all his fights both as amateur and professional, but at 17 fell in with the request of the Kent committee to give up boxing because of the danger of damage to his eyesight.

In the wartime Service matches at Lord's Sgt. Evans attracted favourable attention and with Leslie Ames henceforward playing for Kent only as a batsman there was, in 1946, an immediate place for him in the Kent XI. His first England cap swiftly followed. Evans's keeping was from the first in strong contrast to the quiet, undemonstrative school of Strudwick and Oldfield, the Australian. He was more in the style of George Duckworth, for ever in hostile collaboration with the bowler, the batsman always well aware of his presence. To all but the fastest bowling he stood close behind the stumps. In particular he formed a perfect association with the best of England's post-war bowlers, the fast-medium Alec Bedser. No finer illustration of the art of wicket-keeping could be imagined than his keeping to Bedser on the lively Melbourne pitches of their day.

Evans was almost always at his best on the big occasion, so he was unlucky that one off-day had crucial consequences. At Headingley in 1948 Australia clinched the rubber thanks to a stand of 301 between Morris and Bradman. Both should have been stumped early in their innings, Morris off Compton, Bradman off Laker. The following winter in South Africa, he was dropped for two Tests in favour of S. C. Griffith. Though not always at his best for Kent, his England place was otherwise secure.

The challenge of a difficult situation inspired him both as keeper and as a batsman. In 1950 on a wicked pitch at Old Trafford and going in at a score of 88 for five he made 104 out of a stand with Trevor Bailey of 161. In easier circumstances two years later at Lord's he made another Test hundred against India, 98 of them before lunch. In his best year, 1952, he made 1613 runs at an average of 28. His most famous batting achievement, however, was at Adelaide in 1946–47 to stay in with Denis Compton for 95 minutes before scoring his first run while his partner was repeating his first innings hundred. Together they saved the match.

Evans's bag of 219 Test victims, 173 caught, 46 stumped, was a world record until his Kent successor Alan Knott exceeded it. With the gap of only a few years in the 1960s three Kent 'keepers (Ames, Evans and Knott) wore the gloves for England in 233 Test matches spread over half a century. (Paul Downton, a Kent cap who moved to Middlesex because of Knott's presence and followed him with 30 Test appearances in the 1980s, was the seventh Kent wicket-keeper to play for England.)

In retirement Evans pursued several activities. He was a public relations officer. There were commercial projects wherein his sanguine nature was inclined to lead to difficulties. He traded in inexpensive jewellery. He was a genial pub-keeper, combining that with a job he held for many years advising on the odds for Ladbrokes, the bookmakers, at Test matches. Hidden behind thick whiskers, with his quick, jaunty walk he was nevertheless instantly recognisable. In 1960 he was appointed CBE. In 1973 he married Angela Peart. They had one daughter.

J. W. HEARNE

Best of all the Hearnes

Hearne, John William   Professional

b: Hillingdon, Middlesex, 11 February 1891   *Teams:* Middlesex,
                                                MCC, England

Career batting:
647-1025-116-37252-285*-40.98; hundreds 96-*ct* 348
Bowling: 44926-1839-24.42

Test batting: 24-36-5-806-114-26.00; hundreds 1-*ct* 13
Bowling: 1462-30-48.73

d: West Drayton, Middlesex, 14 September 1965. Aged 74.

John William Hearne was a member of one of the largest and most famous of cricket families, and a cousin of the equally illustrious J.T. After the MCC Australian tour of 1911–12 'Plum' Warner, the captain, wrote of 'Young Jack': 'There is no reason why he should not develop into the best batsman in England. I expect him to be that in five or six years' time. He has a faultless method and is rapidly becoming a powerful driver.' Hearne at this moment had a hundred against Australia to his credit before his 21st birthday. He was, it seemed, on the threshold of great things.

But there came first the Great War and also a deterioration in his health. The very highest promise was not in fact fulfilled. He was often overshadowed, in effect if not in method, by his Middlesex friend and colleague, the more exuberant 'Patsy' Hendren. He never became 'a powerful driver'. Yet in a quiet unassuming way which perfectly expressed his character off the field Jack Hearne remained, until his retirement at the age of 45, an all-round cricketer of great talent and distinction. He reached 1,000 runs 19 times, 5 times also taking 100 wickets. In three of his doubles he scored 2,000 runs. And if he was not again often spectacularly successful in Test matches it should not be forgotten that the record of the 1920-21 MCC team in Australia must have been vastly better if, after a brilliant beginning, his health had not broken down. I must not forget his leg-break bowling. He had sharp powers of spin and that dip in the flight that separates the best from the commonplace. On his day – especially on a slightly dusty wicket – he was as dangerous as anyone.

Hearne and Hendren carried the Middlesex batting on their shoulders almost until the moment that that other great pair, D. C. S. Compton and W. J. Edrich, succeeded them in the later thirties. No county has had a finer quartet than this, nor perhaps two such pairs in succession. Hearne's trim figure, the cap very straight and well pulled down over the nose, sleeves often buttoned at the wrist, will come easily to the memory of the Lord's habitués of his day. His cricket had not only great competence but an unruffleable dignity. The high regard in which the professionals of that generation were held owed indeed as much to him as to anyone.

'TUPPY' OWEN-SMITH

No greater all-round sportsman

Owen-Smith, Dr Harold Geoffrey Owen   Amateur

b: Rondebosch, Cape Town, South Africa, 18 February 1909

Sch: Diocesan College, Rondebosch   *Teams:* Western Province, Oxford U., Middlesex, South Africa

Career batting:
101-162-11-4059-168*-26.88; hundreds 3-*ct* 93
Bowling: 7410-319-23.22

Test batting:
5-8-2-252-129-42.00; hundreds 1-*ct* 4
Bowling: 113-0

d: Rosebank, Cape Town, South Africa, 27 February 1990. Aged 81.

Dr 'Tuppy' Owen-Smith, the prodigiously talented all-round games player, shares with C. B. Van Ryneveld the distinction of having played rugby for England and cricket for South Africa. As a cricketer his finest hour was his brilliant 129 in the third Test against England at Headingley in 1929. The match had seemed to be comfortably won by England – Neville Cardus, covering it for the *Manchester Guardian*, had left the ground on a romantic errand – when Owen-Smith came to the rescue. Only 20 at the time and on his first visit to England, he made 102 before lunch on the last day, and shared in the last-wicket partnership of 103. England were left scrambling for victory, which they eventually achieved thanks to Frank Woolley.

Owen-Smith was educated at Diocesan College, Cape Town. In 1931 he won a Rhodes scholarship to Magdalen College, Oxford. He promptly gained a boxing blue, winning his bout against Cambridge as a welterweight. His next assault on Cambridge was at Lord's, where he and the late Nawab of Pataudi set Oxford on the path to a historic win by making 174 together in an hour and a half. Owen-Smith's wrist-spin then helped to seal the victory. He made an even greater impression at Twickenham, frustrating the brilliant Cambridge runners of the early 1930s in two extraordinary displays of full-back play. Though not heavily built, he was remarkably tough and a fearless tackler.

After Oxford he trained as a doctor in London at St Mary's, where he formed a distinguished link in the hospital's long sporting tradition. When medical duties allowed, he played cricket for R. W. V. Robins's powerful Middlesex side. But he achieved even more renown as England's full-back. Indeed, in one game he seemed to be confronting Wales almost single-handed with his coolness and courage. In all he won ten caps, only once being on the losing side. He was in the England side that achieved a famous victory over the All Blacks in 1936, and the next year he captained England in their first success against the Scots at Murrayfield.

In 1938 Owen-Smith qualified, and returned to South Africa, where he became house-surgeon in Rondebosch-Mowbray hospital at the Cape. When war came he served in the Middle East with the South African Army Medical Corps. Afterwards he returned to general practice at Rondebosch where he spent the rest of his life. His career as a doctor was distinguished. In 1957 he became president of the Cape Western branch of the Medical Association of South Africa, and he was also a member of its federal council. In August 1989 he wrote to the *Daily Telegraph* welcoming the news that an English touring team was to visit South Africa that winter, and deploring the spinelessness of the cricket authorities. Almost the last news of him before his death was of his being allowed to leave the oxygen tent to which he was confined to watch an England-Wales international at Twickenham. He relished England's triumph.

Owen-Smith's cheerful, debonair spirit complemented his games-playing skill. Although C. B. Fry is perhaps the only all-round athlete who could be counted his equal, a more modest legend never existed. He and his wife, Margaret, had two sons, one of whom, Michael, is a well-known South African sporting journalist.

R. W. V. ROBINS

Adventurous in all he did

Robins, Robert Walter Vivian   Amateur

b: Stafford, 3 June 1906

Sch: Highgate   *Teams:* Middlesex, Cambridge U., MCC,
England, Cahn to Argentina, North
America and Bermuda

Career batting:
379-565-39-13884-140-26.39; hundreds 11-*ct* 221
Bowling: 22580-969-23.30

Test batting:
19-27-4-612-108-26.60; hundreds 1-*ct* 12
Bowling: 1758-64-27.46

d: Marylebone, London, 12 December 1968. Aged 62.

Robert Walter Vivian Robins was one of the most vivid and
glamorous cricketers of his generation. He was, too, perhaps
the most imaginative and adventurous captain. Such adjectives as
these may suggest to the younger generation a somewhat unpre-
dictable, if colourful, personality on the field, and such he was. If
he conjured victories out of the least promising situations he occasionally failed, either as player or captain, in situations that
demanded far less of him. For him cricket was a game to be
savoured and enjoyed. Dullness, either in technique or tactics,
was to him a crime, and he fought the safety-first mentality in
every context, as captain of Middlesex and of England, as a Test
selector (for two spells of three years each), in committee-room
and in conversation, and as MCC touring manager. His job in that
capacity in the West Indies in 1959–60 was not the least of his services to the game.

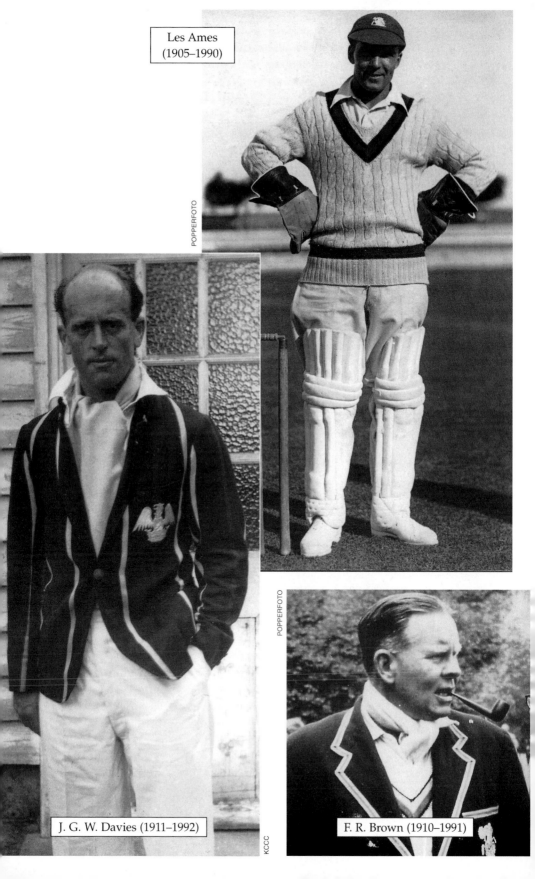

Les Ames
(1905–1990)

POPPERFOTO

POPPERFOTO

J. G. W. Davies (1911–1992)

KCCC

F. R. Brown (1910–1991)

Godfrey Evans (1920–1999)

J. W. Hearne (1891–1965)

'Tuppy' Owen-Smith (1909–1990)

POPPERFOTO

R. W. V. Robins
(1906–1968)

Maurice Tate
(1895–1956)

Frank Woolley (1887–1978)

POPPERFOTO

POPPERFOTO

Rex Alston (1901–1994)

R. C. Robertson-Glasgow
(1901-1965)

H. S. Altham (1888–1965)

John Arlott (1914–1991)

Sir Neville Cardus (1888–1975)

Alan Gibson (1923–1997)

Brian Johnston
(1912–1994)

PATRICK EAGAR

Michael Melford (1916–1999)

Ron Roberts (1927–1965)

'Tich' Freeman
(1888–1965)

Tony Lock
(1929–1995)

J. C. White (1891–1961)

Jim Laker (1922–1986)

Ian Peebles (1908–1980)

Hugh Tayfield (1929–1994)

Doug Wright
(1914–1998)

He had, predictably, a contempt for figures, which were achieved, as it were, in spite of himself. His most notable feats for England were in 1933 when he took six for 32 against the West Indies at Lord's, and his 108 against South Africa at Old Trafford in 1935, made under threat of collapse in just over two hours. His overall figures were not scintillating. Yet he might well be considered the most brilliant all-rounder of his day. If good bowling needed putting in its place here was your man; if a stand needed breaking no one was more likely to do it. (He won the Trent Bridge Test of 1930 by bowling Don Bradman with a googly that the great man left alone.) Above all as a fielder of instinctive reflexes, speed, and nimble all-round skill he was among Englishmen (which is to say excluding only Learie Constantine) the brightest star of his generation. He must have been one of the best cover points in England at the age of 50.

The peak of Robins's career was reached in the years of 1935–38, when his leadership of Middlesex did much to energize the county championship generally. After languishing at the foot of the table for five years, Middlesex under him finished successively 3rd, 2nd, 2nd and 2nd again.

His greatest playing disappointment occurred in this time. Going on his only major MCC tour (he was asked for several more) as vice-captain to G. O. Allen in 1936 he broke the top joint of the second finger of his right hand in the first week, ironically at fielding practice. Thereafter he could neither spin the ball, nor grip the bat properly, yet played in four of the Tests and delighted the crowds with his fielding.

He had his greatest reward after the war when in 1947 he led Middlesex to the Championship that had so narrowly eluded him before. From Highgate, where he was something of a prodigy (206 and seven for 54 v Aldenham on the same day), he got a blue at Cambridge as a freshman. In his third University match he made 53 and 101 not out (in 105 minutes) and took eight wickets. For Middlesex in 1929 he scored 1,134 runs and took 162 wickets, and was first capped for England at Lord's. That was his first and last full season's county cricket, before his seven as captain. In 1966, aged 60, he captained the Cross Arrows at Lord's, 42 years after making 97 in his first innings there, for the Rest against the Lord's Schools.

On the soccer field Robins was a dangerous outside-right, who captained Cambridge, played in League football for Nottingham Forest, and, more notably, was once a member of several of the

Corinthian FA Cup teams that so successfully revived ancient amateur glories in the twenties and thirties.

MAURICE TATE

Legendary fame

Tate, Maurice William   Professional

b: Brighton, Sussex, 30 May 1895

Teams: Sussex, MCC, England

Career batting:
679-970-103-21717-203-25.04; hundreds 23-*ct* 284
Bowling: 50571-2784-18.16

Test batting:
39-52-5-1198-100*-25.48; hundreds 1-*ct* 11
Bowling: 4055-155-26.16

d: Wadhurst, Sussex, 18 May 1956. Aged 60.

Maurice Tate was one of the greatest English all-round crick-eters between the two wars. He figured in 20 consecutive Tests against Australia from 1924–25 and took more wickets in a series against Australia than any other bowler. (His 38 wickets at a cost of 23 runs each has since been bettered by Jim Laker with 46 and Sir Alec Bedser with 39.) In 1927, his best season with the bat, he scored 1,713 runs, including five hundreds.

Maurice Tate was the son of Fred Tate, who himself took 1,306 wickets for Sussex. In 1922 Maurice proved himself among the best all-rounders in the country by taking 118 wickets and scoring almost 1,000 runs. He was later to complete the double of 100 wickets and 1,000 runs eight times. Following his retirement in 1937 he kept several inns in Sussex and for some years was cricket coach at Tonbridge School. In 1949 he became an honorary member of the MCC.

Maurice Tate is a legendary name in English cricket. His sudden death came as a shock, for only three weeks before those present at Arundel, and who watched the match between the Duke of Norfolk's XI and the Australians on their TV screens, will have seen him officiating as umpire. He began as a batsman and burst suddenly upon the world as a bowler at the age of 27. Between 1924 and 1930 he was England's leading bowler, and he continued to play with distinction for Sussex until 1937, when he was 42. His pace was distinctly on the quick side of medium, and his virtues, based on the smoothest, most economical of actions, included added pace off the ground and the ability to swing the ball late either way. He was a pioneer of the style that has come since to be called 'seam' bowling, in which his most distinguished successor has been Sir Alec Bedser. Those who watched him in Australia under the leadership of his county captain, A. E. R. Gilligan, in 1924–25, when he took 38 Test wickets in the series, assert that no finer bowling of its type has ever been seen.

Maurice was a true son of Sussex, a simple, genial, most like-able man, with genius in that swing of the hips and shoulders and the piston motion of his strong right arm.

FRANK WOOLLEY

One of the immortals

Woolley, Frank Edward   Professional

b: Tonbridge, Kent, 27 May 1887

Sch: Wesleyan School, Tonbridge   *Teams:* Kent, MCC, England

Career batting:
978-1530-84-58969-305*-40.77; hundreds 145-*ct* 1018
Bowling: 41058-2068-19.87

Test batting: 64-98-7-3283-154-36.07; hundreds 5-*ct* 64
Bowling: 2815-83-33.91

d: Halifax, Nova Scotia, Canada, 18 October 1978. Aged 91.

Frank Woolley was one of the great cricketers of history and in particular the pride of Kent. He was as graceful a batsman as ever played. The beauty of his batting was despite a quite apparent stiffness of limb and gait. As with Denis Compton, one tended not to notice a certain awkwardness of movement in the joyous contemplation of the stroke. Familiarity and affection breed a blindness to such detail. And if, coldly analysed, he was hardly a graceful figure, he was a supremely rhythmic, stylish, debonair striker of a cricket ball.

Charm is a difficult virtue to dissect. The late R. C. Robertson-Glasgow began his 'Print' of Frank Woolley, in that delightful series of his, by saying that 'he was easy to watch, difficult to bowl to, and impossible to write about'. The key to his play, as with all the very greatest, was an extraordinary refinement of timing and that again seemed to derive from the severe simplicity and correctness of his method. Here was this extremely tall, slim figure, swinging his bat in the fullest and truest pendulum through the line of the ball. There were no kinks or ornamentations – no one surely was ever so free from mannerism. Here comes the ball, there goes the foot, down she comes and through. Naturally enough Woolley was a glorious driver, while to the shorter straight one he played a perpendicular back stroke with a power which could be generated from the easiest, laziest swing. But of the more delicate strokes he was equally the master, and here was to be seen his amazing keeness of eye. He was a glorious cutter, and no one turned the ball more finely and prettily off his legs.

Such is a brief technical appraisal of his batsmanship, but what endeared him to the ringside, and at the same time made him so devastating an opponent, was his whole approach to batsmanship. The modest, self-effacing companion of the dressing-room quickly became an utterly disdainful, aloof antagonist at the wicket. Robertson-Glasgow, in his article, went on to say that Frank Woolley was never known to express a particular liking or distaste for any bowler. He seemed superbly indifferent to who was bowling, or how they were bowling. He sometimes got out, I believe, because he had refused to recognise a particular trap set for him. He certainly paid the penalty, now and then, for taking to himself a bowler whom a comrade did not relish, seeking to knock him off. The thing he never seemed to contemplate, let alone to fear, was getting out himself. He was the antithesis of the calculating, bread-and-butter run collector. He played the ball on its merits and he played for his side.

In the nineties he batted precisely, as he would bat after the century was reached. He was a Kentish cricketer of the county's golden age. In his first year, as a lad of 19 in 1906, he played with K. L. Hutchings, J. R. Mason, C. J. Burnup, and R. N. R. Blaker in the team that first brought the championship to Kent. 'We were never allowed to play for averages in the Kent side,' he wrote in *Wisden* on his retirement, and went on to say that it was never the policy that the pitch must be occupied all day after winning the toss. Such was his early environment, the influence of which so firmly shaped his attitude throughout his cricket life.

As to his bowling, I have not attempted a description, for his serious efforts ended in the early twenties, and I have only the memory of an occasional over, of the easy slanting run, left hand behind the back, and the poise of the high action. But it is as well to remember that before the 1914–18 war he was not only the best all-rounder in England but very nearly the best slow left-arm bowler; likewise, too, and right up to middle age, one of the finest of slip fieldsmen. He took 1,018 catches, more than any man. He cared little for figures; yet only Jack Hobbs narrowly bettered his aggregate of 58,969 runs (including 145 hundreds). Only 26 bowlers have taken more than his 2,068 wickets.

Many of the innings one has seen from him come readily to mind in kaleidoscope: two brief but perfect gems at Lord's, both, oddly enough, of 41 runs, one against Australia in the second Test of Bradman's first tour, the other his farewell in Gentlemen and Players match at the age of 51; several prolonged and severe chastisements of the Champion County bowlers at The Oval – he averaged a hundred in this annual fixture; a lovely piece of play that enriched a cold Trial match at Old Trafford wherein, aged 45 and going in first, he punished Larwood and Voce for 50 runs within the hour; and for Kent, a century before lunch against Nottinghamshire at Canterbury after rain, on a nasty, lifting pitch. Alas! that one knows so many of the greatest only at second hand, notably the classic 95 and 93 at Lord's in 1921 against Armstrong's Australians, in his own view the two best innings he ever played.

He was quite active into his late eighties and in January 1971 flew to Australia to watch the last two Tests. Aged 84, he married for a second time, his first wife having died ten years earlier. His second bride was Mrs Martha Morse, an American widow, to whom he introduced the pleasures of Canterbury Week.

9

COMMUNICATORS

REX ALSTON

Washed in a cold bath

Alston, Arthur Reginald

b: Faringdon, Berkshire, 2 July 1901

sch: Trent College

d: Ewhurst, Surrey, 8 September 1994. Aged 93.

R ex Alston was a household name in sports broadcasting during the two decades after the Second World War. He seemed
equally at home describing cricket at Lord's, rugby football at
Twickenham, lawn tennis at Wimbledon or athletics at the White
City. In each of these roles Alston came across as a precise, consci-
entious, fair-minded commentator, aspiring to no heights of
imagery but concerned to convey to the listener a clear and accurate picture. His voice and style were as far as possible removed
from the Hampshire burr and imaginative word-pictures of an
Arlott or the jokey pleasantries of a Johnston; and for some his
stints on the air made an agreeable contrast.

On three of his four subjects Alston had the advantage of speaking from first-hand knowledge. At cricket he was a Cambridge
Crusader, before playing six seasons for Bedfordshire, whom he
captained in the Minor Counties' Championship in 1932. He
played rugby football on the wing for Bedford, East Midlands and
Rosslyn Park, and he gained an athletics half-blue, running second in the 100 yards to Harold Abrahams in the university sports,
and helping Oxford and Cambridge to beat Harvard and Yale at
Wembley in 1923. There is no record of Alston achieving any
notable skill at tennis, but for many years he did a capable job in
the Wimbledon Championships beside Max Robertson and Dan
Maskell.

Alston covered four Olympic Games for the BBC – from

189

London in 1948 to Tokyo in 1964 – generally in partnership with Abrahams. His most memorable broadcast was of the great race in the Commonwealth Games between Roger Bannister and the Australian John Landy, who were then the only men to have broken the four-minute barrier. All who listened will recall Alston crying 'He can't do it!' as Landy led round the last bend – to be followed, as Bannister swept past with that wonderful finishing burst, with 'He's done it!'

The son of the Rt. Rev. A. F. Alston, Suffragan Bishop of Middleton, Arthur Reginald Alston was born on 2 July 1901 and educated at Trent and Clare College, Cambridge. He began as an assistant master at Bedford, where he ran the cricket. In 1941, after being rejected for call-up on grounds of age (he was then 40), he was persuaded by the musician Leslie Woodgate to join the BBC as a billeting officer.

At the end of the Second World War S. J. 'Lobby' de Lotbinière, the head of Outside Broadcasts, appointed Alston to 'a job which was heaven-sent for me'. He was put in charge of the outside broadcasting of the four sports with which he became identified.

Except when Wimbledon or athletics claimed his attention Arlott, Alston and myself were the resident Test Match broadcasters in the early post-war years. Alston commentated on more than a hundred Tests, including those when he toured Australia, West Indies and South Africa as the BBC representative. He covered nearly as many rugby internationals. He had an unnerving experience in Trinidad when a riot caused play to be suspended. Believing Alston guilty of an insensitive remark, the crowd hurled bottles at the commentary box until the police intervened.

Alston's years as a schoolmaster made him a rare stickler for accuracy. He would hurriedly correct himself even when there was little chance of the listener being able to spot, say, a case of mistaken identity in the field. Once towards the end of his time he got into a muddle amusing to everyone other than himself. There was a Pakistani player whose name, Afaq Hussain, made commentators understandably nervous. According to Brian Johnston's version Alston announced: 'There's going to be a change of bowling. We're going to see Afaq to Knight at the pavilion end.' Whereupon Alston held his head in his hands and said: 'What am I saying? He isn't even playing.'

Alston reached retirement age in 1961, but continued to broadcast long after that as a freelance. He also reported on cricket and rugby for the *Daily Telegraph* and the *Sunday Telegraph*. He published *Taking the Air* (1950), *Over to Rex Alston* (1953), *Test Commentary* (1956) and *Watching Cricket* (1962).

In 1985 – by one of those unhappy mischances that are the obituarist's nightmare – *The Times* managed to publish his obituary notice. Alston complained that it was not only premature but incomplete. Alston's first wife, Elspeth, daughter of Sir Stewart Stockman, had died earlier that year. In 1986 *The Times* was given the opportunity to reassure Alston's admirers by publishing the news of his second marriage to Joan Wilson. Alston, still trim of figure and with his pleasant light voice unchanged, continued to report games until the mid-1980s. He gave as his secret the fact that he *washed* daily in a cold bath.

H. S. ALTHAM AND
R. C. ROBERTSON-GLASGOW

Scholar-sportsmen

Altham, Harry Surtees, CBE, DSO, MC   Amateur

b: Camberley, Surrey, 30 November 1888

Sch: Repton   *Teams:* Oxford U., Surrey, Hampshire

Career batting:
55-87-9-1537-141-19.70; hundreds 1-*ct* 26
Bowling: 47-0

d: Fulwood, Sheffield, Yorkshire, 11 March 1965. Aged 76.

Robertson-Glasgow, Raymond Charles   Amateur

b: Murrayfield, Edinburgh, Scotland, 15 July 1901

Sch: Charterhouse   *Teams:* Oxford U., Somerset

Career batting:
144-223-64-2102-80-13.22; *ct* 88
Bowling: 11959-464-25.77

d: Buckhold, Berkshire, 4 March 1965. Aged 63.

It is axiomatic that a game reflects the character of those who play and those who serve it. By this token cricket is made infinitely poorer by the deaths within a few days of one another in March 1965 of H. S. Altham and R. C. Robertson-Glasgow. In personality so unlike, they had so much in common that they were inevitably close friends. Both were scholars, Raymond – or 'Crusoe' as he was generally known in the cricket world – literally so of his college, Corpus Christi. Both were cricketers of distinction, both schoolmasters, though 'Crusoe's' health was the cause of his turning quite early from teaching to games-writing. That, of course, was a talent they shared in a high degree, and uniquely wide as was the scope of Harry Altham's contributions to the game it is probably as a historian that he will be best remembered.

Both in their separate styles were in the highest class of after-dinner speakers, and while in late life 'Crusoe' was on doctor's orders forbidden to indulge his wit and whimsical fancy in this way, Harry's astonishing zest led him to undertake more than he should have done. It was not in his nature to ease up. He hated to say no to any request in connection with cricket, and I suppose that the manner of his death, after speaking at a cricket dinner, will have been very much as his friends would have foretold. Both these old blues were devoted in particular to Oxford cricket and the Parks, where in the spring those University sides whose captains were wise enough to invite them there were sure to profit from their advice. In the thirties their visitations often coincided, and the fortunate undergraduates might turn from the kind, encouraging, dedicated coaching of the one to the light-hearted, not to say at times ribald, comment of the other.

H.S.A., of course, was the complete mentor, but 'Crusoe' was a particular help to bowlers, especially the faster ones of his own kind, as many a now middle-aged cricketer will testify. Both perhaps were altogether at their best and happiest with the young in any sort of context. Harry's interest in an encouragement of the Winchester racket players was second only to his involvement in the school's cricket: and to how many has he not brought an appreciation of things ecclesiastical by his tours of Winchester Cathedral, on which he was perhaps the leading authority? Who of St Andrew's School, Pangbourne, in the grounds of which 'Crusoe' lived for the last twenty years of his life, will not remember his brilliant, highly individual conduct of the Litt. Soc.?

Both, incidentally, have been among the most distinguished contributors to *The Cricketer* ever since the paper was founded in 1921. Harry's *History of Cricket* first appeared there in serial form in this paper in the early twenties: how he found time for the research and the writing, leading the busy life of a Winchester don, and playing for Hampshire and the Harlequins in August, is one of the minor miracles.

Both fulfilled for me every test of friendship over a span of well over thirty years. I first got to know Harry on the cricket field, playing against him when the Harlequins came to the Saffrons on their August tour. He managed and led the Harlequins, and to observe him in either capacity was an education to a young cricketer: much fun, infinite good humour, but always the fullest rigour of the game: no half-hearted performer, inclined to slackness, would have lasted a second match with him.

In 1937 Harry asked me, to my great joy, to undertake the new work on the second edition of *A History of Cricket*, and since then we had been associated closely not only in the subsequent editions but in other ventures, not least *The World of Cricket*, to which he contributed some superb biographical sketches of the great. I had not supposed he would want to be plagued with much work on this new venture, until I found him almost offended at not having been asked to do more. In the end, to the inestimable advantage of the book, he wrote some 30,000 words. Such was his energy and unimpaired enthusiasm.

When he retired from regular teaching at the end of the forties he probably became even busier than before: his life revolved now around Winchester and Lord's. The Treasurership of MCC, involving ex-officio membership of all committees, made the most exacting demands, as also did the MCC Youth Cricket Association. This was very largely his brainchild, the germ of the idea coming, I believe, from a correspondence in the *Daily Telegraph* following the triumphal tour of the 1948 Australians, with its clear message to English cricket. He was the inspiration right up to his death of the coaching courses run by the MCC YCA, at Lilleshall.

The tragic key to 'Crusoe's' life was the acute mental depression that plagued him in black, inevitable cycles, alternating with the moods of exaltation and mental brilliance when all his best work was done, and when he was the most scintillating company in the world. This half of him was all that most were permitted to see, and it is by this that he will be remembered. 'Crusoe' batting, arms crossed, with a surf-board on the sands at Jersey; 'Crusoe' going in number 11 to save the match for Somerset at Fenner's, entering the field from the press-box at square-leg where he had been shaping his light report for the *Morning Post*, and being stumped by a mile; above all, perhaps, 'Crusoe' on many a summer's evening among the tankards at Vincent's Club holding forth with a spontaneity wonderfully diverse on any subject under the sun. 'Here's Crusoe,' everyone would say wherever cricketers gathered, 'now for some fun!' He never disappointed, but few knew at what cost. He, like Harry Altham in a rather different way, was very much the victim of his friends.

In one of the 25-word letters which as PoWs we were allowed, I received from him in a Thai jungle the information that he had married a fine Scottish widow named Elizabeth Hutton. She devoted herself to Crusoe's care – as indeed Alison Altham did for H.S.A. There is still a selective demand for Crusoe's books, notably the *Cricket Prints* and his autobiography *46 Not Out*.

JOHN ARLOTT
Voice of cricket

Arlott, Leslie Thomas John, OBE

b: Basingstoke, Hampshire, 25 February 1914

Sch: Queen Mary's GS, Basingstoke

d: Alderney, 14 December 1991. Aged 77.

John Arlott turned the routine business of cricket commentary into something approaching an art form, so that for 34 years his rich and mellow Hampshire tones became an integral part of the English summer. His style was instantly recognisable not merely by the accent but also by an incomparable blend of poetic imagination, verbal resource, shrewd judgment of character, and ready humour. Arlott was essentially an impressionist, with an eye for the telling irrelevancy; he never descended into mere punditry.

As a phrase-maker he was unmatched. 'Consider Lillee in the field,' he once observed. 'He toils mightily but he does not spin.' Lillee, incidentally, claimed that it was listening to Arlott that had first made him interested in cricket: 'He really made me want to play.' An authority of another kind, Dylan Thomas, described Arlott's commentaries as 'exact, enthusiastic, prejudiced, amazingly visual, authoritative and friendly'. Apart from the quality of his broadcasts, he stood alone in sheer volume of output. From the first Test of 1946 against India at Lord's he covered an unbroken succession of Tests at home until he retired after the Centenary Test against Australia in 1980. He also commentated on Sunday League games for television, although he never seemed quite at home in a medium that obviated the necessity for word painting. Arlott signed off for the last time as though it were a normal occasion – 'and now, after comment by Trevor Bailey, it will be Christopher Martin-Jenkins.' But first his fellow commentators, then (after a loudspeaker announcement) the fielding Australian side and the entire Lord's crowd, stood and applauded him – a gesture that was almost too much for this deeply emotional man.

Arlott reverenced the gods of cricket, in particular Sir Jack Hobbs, in whose honour he founded the Master's Club, which still meets occasionally, its membership refreshed by selected lovers of the game. He delighted to celebrate the journeymen of cricket, forgotten players like Jack Mercer, who represented Glamorgan from 1922 to 1939 and 'bowled more overs, conceded more runs, took more wickets, scored the fastest 50, made more ducks and was Not Out more often than anyone else in the county's history'.

Arlott loved the fellowship of cricket, and held the players, as a group, in rare esteem. His warm feelings were reciprocated, and the distinction which probably meant more to him than any other was his presidency of the Cricketers' Association, now the Professional Cricketers' Association. His part in steering this professional players' trade union from its foundation to its present position of respect within the game reflected his concern for them.

John was a self-made man of letters, a passionate collector of books, aquatints and glass, a Liberal candidate (at Epping in 1955 and 1959), a lover of France and above all, an oenophile strong on theory and even stronger in practice. At first he showed a marked partiality for sherry, but next came a consuming appreciation of claret and champagne followed by burgundy. He became wine correspondent for the *Evening News*, learning as he drank, one might say. When on retirement he moved from Alresford to Alderney, the head of Christie's wine department said his was the finest collection he had ever handled. A headline announced, 'Arlott declares at 4,000 bottles.' Among his friends his capacity was a legend.

His other interests meant that for him the loss of a Test series, far from being a national catastrophe, was simply another phase in the history of a game which existed in the last analysis simply for the purposes of entertainment. But this kind of awareness also implied a reciprocal responsibility. Arlott had been shocked by what he saw in South Africa when covering MCC's tour of 1948–49, and thenceforth he fiercely opposed any suggestion that cricket should lend itself to the sustenance of apartheid. He condemned players on the unofficial tour of 1982 as 'cynical, mercenary and completely selfish'. Conversely, he regarded the part he had played in bringing Basil D'Oliveira to England as the most important thing that he ever did.

John Arlott was born in the Basingstoke lodge of the cemetery where his grandfather had been registrar. He won a charity scholarship to Queen Mary's Grammar School. Here he nurtured a deep loathing for the caning headmaster, who had decreed that the young Arlott should never play for the school again after being convicted of violent play in a football match. In 1926 he went to The Oval to watch the first day of the Test match against Australia, so conceiving his devotion to Hobbs. Arlott's love of cricket was further developed by his reading of Neville Cardus's *The Summer Game,* which afforded the first intimations that cricket might serve as a medium for descriptive genius.

He began his working career, however, as office boy to the Basingstoke town planning officer and then became diet clerk at the local mental hospital. In 1934 he joined the police force, and after a spell in the tough training school at Birmingham, went on the beat in Southampton. He watched Hampshire play whenever he could, and on one occasion his wildest fantasies were fulfilled when, in an emergency, he was asked to field (in borrowed flannels) for the county against Worcestershire. During the Blitz he was appointed to the War Emergency Department, and then – having acquired a smattering of Norwegian and German to go with his French – he found himself translated into Detective Constable, Special Branch.

His literary pretensions had a breakthrough when John Betjeman mentioned the phenomenon of the 'policeman-poet' to Geoffrey Grigson, then a talks producer with the BBC at Bristol, who proceeded to commission a talk from the prodigy. Arlott huffily replied that he was not prepared to be exhibited as a freak, but agreed, nevertheless, to present himself for an audition. Grigson noted in his report, 'This man is a natural broadcaster and should be encouraged.'

Required to give further evidence of his abilities, Arlott wrote a piece entitled 'The Hampshire Giants', about Hambledon Cricket Club. Its broadcast constituted Arlott's debut alike as a broadcaster and as a cricket expert. Subsequently he was offered the chance to compere a programme of *Country Magazine,* and in 1945 he applied for and secured the job of literary programmes producer, Overseas Services, in London. Arlott was put in charge of two weekly programmes, one of poetry and one of prose. He produced the poetry programme *Book of Verse* for more than four years, working with many literary luminaries.

Then, in January 1946, Donald Stevenson, head of the BBC Eastern Service, asked Arlott to broadcast short (and unpaid) reports of the Indian touring team's first two matches. These transmissions were deemed so successful that Arlott was commissioned to persist with them throughout the summer. From then on all was plain sailing.

SIR NEVILLE CARDUS

Symphonies in words

Cardus, Sir Neville, CBE

b: Rusholme, Manchester, 2 April 1888

Sch: A Manchester board school

d: London, 28 February 1975. Aged 86.

Distinguished cricket writer and music critic of the *Manchester Guardian* and contributor both to the *Sunday Times* and the *Sydney Morning Herald*, Cardus achieved a unique reputation by reporting cricket in a colourful and often humorous prose style not known hitherto. Writing first above the pseudonym Cricketer, he brought new devotees to the game after the First World War, just as John Arlott did by the medium of radio after the Second. In his *Dictionary of National Biography* notice Michael Kennedy wrote that Cardus 'was more interested in aesthetics than technicalities, in emotions rather than intellectual response'. So he was – *much* more. He thought that one of his best reports was of the last day of the 1929 Headingley Test against South Africa, of which he saw not a ball bowled since he was pursuing an affair of the heart far away in Surrey.

I did not write a formal obituary, but readers may catch the flavour of Cardus and his work from my report of his Memorial Service. The occasion, at St Paul's, Covent Garden – a church long associated with the arts – reflected in its complete originality both the genius of the man and a philosophical stance which had advanced significantly from the atheism of his youth.

John Hester, priest-in-charge of St Paul's and rector of St Anne's, Soho, in his brief introduction to the service, quoted Cardus as subscribing to the adjuration of Jowett, the famous Master of Balliol, to the young Margot Asquith: 'You must believe in God, my dear, despite what the clergy tell you.' After this there was little but the Cross and candles, and the white light over the aumbry to remind us that we were in church. The Royal Philharmonic Orchestra, conducted by James Loughran of the Hallé, gave us Elgar's Serenade for Strings, and movements from two concertos by Mozart, these interspersed by Alan Gibson's address and readings by Dame Flora Robson, Wendy Hiller, and David Gray, of the *Guardian*.

Poor Mr Gibson got off to an unlucky start, for when it seemed the conductor had declared his first innings and the speaker accordingly mounted the pulpit, the music suddenly burst out again and he had to return to the dressing-room. However, it takes more than this to put Mr Gibson off his stride, and he was soon pencilling in with subtle strokes an affectionate portrait of the essential Cardus. He spoke as one of many brought to an appreciation of the game by his subject, in his case by *Good Days* with its immortal passage on Emmott Robinson, for Neville the incarnation of Yorkshire:

> Robinson seemed to be made out of the stuff of Yorkshire county; I imagine that the Lord one day gathered together a heap of Yorkshire clay and breathed into it and said, 'Emmott Robinson, go on and bowl at the pavilion end for Yorkshire.' He looked the old soldier, with his lined face and fine grey hairs. He shambled about the field with his trousers loose. You were getting ready to see them fall down altogether when he would remember them in time.

Alan Gibson wearing his Oxford hood ought to be on permanent call for occasions such as this. He suggested that William Blake's lines might express Cardus's philosophy as personified in his writing: 'Man was made for Joy and Woe; And when this we rightly know, Thro' the world we safely go, Joy and Woe are woven fine, A clothing for the soul divine.'

He wasn't sure that Cardus would agree with Blake, 'but anyway he's probably busy just now, arguing with Bernard Shaw'. From Dame Flora we had a Shakespeare sonnet, from Miss Hiller the famous lines of Francis Thompson's 'At Lord's' with a special anguish reserved for the concluding lament, 'Oh, my Hornby and my Barlow long ago.' Mr Gray had found some appropriate metaphysical passages from *Second Innings*.

All the foremost institutions in cricket and music with which Cardus was identified were represented. There was such a strong sardonic side to Neville that one could not be sure how much he would have approved of such a gathering. Yet if there be doubt of that it was for us who paid tribute a satisfaction as well as a duty. I suppose many came away feeling, as I did, that though some of us by our work may have held the attention of those brought up to an interest in cricket he introduced the game into countless lives which but for his unique skill would never have known it.

ALAN GIBSON

Wit and humour through the dullest day

Gibson, Norman Alan Stewart

b: Sheffield, 20 May 1923

Sch: Monoux GS and Taunton

d: Taunton, 10 April 1997. Aged 73.

A lan Gibson, the journalist, author and broadcaster, was a fond figure in the world of cricket. He was also a poet, BBC producer, historian, lay preacher, and active Liberal. An all-round man, indeed, in the tradition of E. V. Lucas, Robertson-Glasgow and Arlott. His cricket writing was to be found at various stages in *The Times*, the *Sunday Telegraph*, the *Guardian*, the *Spectator* and *The Cricketer*. His books include *Cricket Captains of England* (1979) and an autobiography, *A Mingled Yarn* (1976), in which cricket is a recurring theme.

Gibson broadcast a little Test cricket, but these ponderous battles were too solemn for his taste and, as a freelance, he found himself writing and talking chiefly about the county game. His genius lay in drawing a thread of wit and humour through the dullest day's play. Thus he repaid editors who allowed him a degree of licence. He might dilate on the plumbing arrangements at Cheltenham or some ripe gossip from the beer tent. As a West Countryman frequently required to journey east by train, he was forever getting stranded at Didcot. One could not imagine either him or his idol, Raymond Robertson-Glasgow, doing anything nearly as practical as driving a car. What they both had the power to do was reduce their readers to open laughter. Gibson's 'Journals of the Season' in Autumn numbers of *The Cricketer* were as consistently funny as anything written about the game.

Gibson was born at Sheffield. His father had started work in the mines at Spennymoor, Co. Durham, at the age of 12, but educated himself sufficiently to be admitted to Spurgeon's College, the training place for the Baptist ministry. In the First World War he was commissioned into the Durham Light Infantry. His son described him, in Milton's understanding of the word, as a saint. Gibson's mother was a rigid Methodist, strong on abstinence. So was Gibson, in his adolescence. He spent his boyhood years first at Ilkley and then at Leyton in a house overlooking the then Essex county ground. Hence the addiction to cricket. From Monoux Grammar School his father, straining the budget, entered him for Taunton School, whence he won an exhibition to Queen's College, Oxford. His university career was interrupted by military arrest when he carelessly cut a medical examination and so spent a brief service chiefly in hospital before being rejected. Never a fit man, he returned to take up the Presidency of the Union and (as he described it) to 'scramble' a First in History. Membership of that vintage post-war Oxford generation was the making of him.

From Oxford, Gibson became a travelling lecturer on the staff of University College, Exeter, but, after marriage and fatherhood, found financial security on the staff of the BBC, West Region, with a wide variety of functions, under Frank Gillard. Still a Baptist lay preacher, though no longer an abstainer ('I took to beer like a brother'), and a Liberal speaker, the ambitious young broadcaster overstretched a dubious physique and precipitated the depressions which, as with 'Crusoe' Robertson-Glasgow, came to dog his life. He was the victim of his own versatility and nervous energy.

From 1968 he combined freelance broadcasting with regular cricket writing for *The Times*. There was also the reporting of rugby football, in print and on the air, and years as an early-morning disc jockey. *Sunday Half-Hour* and *Round Britain Quiz* were also regular chores. In later years, it all became too much. There is a moving chapter in *A Mingled Yarn* on life in a mental hospital.

A happier memory is of Gibson at Sir Neville Cardus's memorial service, his usual casual dress transformed, as he mounted the pulpit wearing the gown and red and black hood of an MA Oxon. Surrounded by the Royal Philharmonic Orchestra he took his text from William Blake.

Joy and woe are woven fine,
A clothing for the soul divine;
Under every grief and pine
Runs a thread of silken twine.

'On an occasion such as this, joy and woe are inseparable companions: thanksgiving for such a life, sadness that it has ended. But more than that: it was the mingling of joy and woe that made Sir Neville such a writer – the sensitivity to the human condition, not least his own.' The epitaph might have been his.

He married first, in 1948, Olwen Thomas; they had two sons. He married secondly, in 1968, Rosemary King; they had a son and daughter. Both marriages were dissolved.

BRIAN JOHNSTON
Ubiquitous and unique

Johnston, Brian Alexander, CBE, MC

b: Hertfordshire, 24 June 1912

Sch: Eton

d: St John's Wood, London, 5 January 1994. Aged 81.

Brian Johnston, the broadcaster, author and entertainer, became both a name and a voice familiar to millions in Britain as well as in cricket-loving countries able to tune in to BBC Radio's *Test Match Special*. Although 'Johnners' was chiefly celebrated as a cricket commentator, many who never followed the summer game knew him from his appearances on such radio shows as *Down Your Way* and *In Town Tonight*, or for providing the commentary on a number of state occasions. Others delighted in his hilarious stage and after-dinner performances, which went a long way to assuage his frustration that he had not become a comedian on the music-halls. Johnston's commentaries were lively, enthusiastic, amusing and informative, and cricket fans in particular enjoyed the sound of his cheerful voice, associated for so many years with the noise of the cricket crowd or the sound of the willow striking the leather ball.

'Johnners' always seemed to be enjoying it all himself – sometimes almost too much so, as when he collapsed into giggles over schoolboyish innuendoes – but below the façade of the enthusiastic amateur lay a complete professional. He joined the BBC staff in 1945 and officially retired in 1972, but remained a phenomenally busy freelance until the end of his life.

Brian Johnston was the youngest of four children of Lt. Col. C. E. Johnston, a City merchant whose coffee business, founded in 1842, enabled the family to live well. Young Brian spent a happy childhood in a beautiful Queen Anne house in Hertfordshire. His interest in cricket began at his preparatory school, Temple Grove, where one of his reports noted that he 'talks too much in school'. He was elected to 'Pop' at Eton, played in the rugby football XV and kept wicket for the XXII (2nd XI). His friends included Jo Grimond and William Douglas Home, whom Johnston recalled excelling himself in an English exam; asked to write briefly on the future of coal, 'he wrote just one word, "smoke", and was awarded seven out of ten'.

At New College, Oxford, Johnston notionally read history, but devoted most of his energies to games, parties and collecting the sort of jokes which amused him for life – such as the *Oxford Mail* headline when Commemoration Balls were cancelled one year: 'Undergraduates Scratch Balls'. On coming down Johnston entered the coffee business. The family firm was now a public company, and although his duties took him away from the City to both Hamburg and Santos he really wanted to be an actor, or at least something in the entertainment world. When in London he frequented the theatre, particularly music-halls such as the old Holborn Empire. The coffee world was not for him. Meantime he played as much cricket as possible, often for the Eton Ramblers.

During the Second World War Johnston was commissioned into the Grenadier Guards. He became technical adjutant of the 2nd Battalion and served in the North-West Europe campaign, winning an MC in 1945. Afterwards he landed a job on the BBC's wireless outside broadcasts team and was immediately in his element. He provided remarkably fluent commentary for live relays of shows direct from a theatre and would interview the stars with great panache and bonhomie. A good mixer with people of all types, he established himself as a top-class interviewer. Further good fortune was to follow.

He was then recruited for the new medium of television and he and I became established in the televised cricket commentary team for next 20-odd years. Yet only a small percentage of Johnston's time was given to cricket. He took over a spot in *In Town Tonight* called 'On the Job' and later tackled the feature 'Let's Go Somewhere' in the same programme. This entailed visiting a wide variety of people and places from the Chamber of Horrors at Madame Tussaud's to the Crazy Gang at the Victoria Palace. In more serious vein, Johnston commentated at King George VI's funeral in 1952, at the Queen's coronation in 1953 and at a number of royal weddings. He contributed to a wide range of radio and television programmes, including *Twenty Questions, Today, What's New?, Sporting Chance* and many others.

In 1963 Johnston was appointed the first-ever BBC cricket correspondent and from then on his broadcasting life was concentrated more on Lord's, near his London home. Until his official retirement from the BBC in 1972 he toured with MCC teams and covered all Test matches at home and abroad. To his chagrin, he was eventually dropped from television commentary when it was decided to concentrate more on former professional cricketers for that medium. But television's loss was radio's gain – and he enjoyed an Indian summer with the ever-popular *Test Match Special* team. He also took on the long-established *Down Your Way* programme and gave it his special cheery stamp until 1987. He was appointed OBE in 1983 and CBE in 1991. His awards included Radio Sports Personality of the Year in 1983. In 1988 he was made President of the Forty Club and he was also an active worker for the Lord's Taverners' charities.

His numerous publications included 13 books on cricket – *It's a Funny Game, Stumped for a Tale, Armchair Cricket* – and a jolly autobiography, characteristically entitled *It's Been a Lot of Fun*, as well as several collections of his jokes, such as *Rain Stops Play* and *Now Here's a Funny Thing*.

'Johnners's' charm was that he never quite grew up. He told good bad jokes which, with his quick delivery and expert timing, were inimitable. He achieved remarkable success doing so many things he enjoyed for so long.

The sadness was that in the last months of his life he accepted too many – over 30 – solo performances in theatres countrywide. They were highly amusing *ad lib* monologues – but an inevitable strain on an octogenarian.

He married, in 1948, Pauline, daughter of Col. William Tozer; they had three sons and two daughters.

MICHAEL MELFORD

He saw sport in perspective

Melford, Michael Austin

b: St John's Wood, London, 9 November 1916

Sch: Charterhouse

d: High Wycombe, 18 April 1999. Aged 82.

Michael Melford was chief cricket and rugby football correspondent for the *Sunday Telegraph* from its foundation in 1961 to 1975, when he succeeded me as cricket correspondent of the *Daily Telegraph*. Melford had first joined the *Daily Telegraph* in 1950, and was in the forefront of the writers who re-established the breadth and quality of the paper's sports pages as the post-war newsprint restrictions were gradually eased. He worked for one or both of the *Telegraphs* for 32 years, and after his retirement in 1982 contributed obituaries until his health began to fail in 1996.

There was a whimsical charm and wit about Melford's writing which appealed to games players and to all who saw sport as a civilised ingredient of life as distinct from a consuming passion. He was wary of superlatives. No hero was hoisted on too lofty a pedestal; and there was generally consolation for the unlucky, whether a team or an individual. He saw games through the eye of the player as well as the spectator. Yet his relaxed philosophy did not prevent him from being severely critical if roused by selfishness or unsporting behaviour. In August 1967, for example, he was outraged by the last day's play of a match between Warwickshire and Yorkshire at Edgbaston.

'Yorkshire clung to the points that they earn for a draw,' his report began, 'but they and their followers are unlikely to look back with pride on the petty, unworthy performance that led to their being booed off the field here this evening.' Melford's detailed criticism of Yorkshire's delaying tactics, which were also described and deplored in *The Times*, carried such authority that MCC admonished Brian Close, the Yorkshire captain, and, after his failure to apologise, removed him from the captaincy of England for the forthcoming tour of the West Indies.

Michael Melford was born at St John's Wood, London. He was the son of Austin Melford, an all-round man of the theatre and a star of the Co-optimists, who, under David Burnaby, successfully revived the old seaside Pierrot show at the Apollo Theatre in the West End during the 1920s. At Charterhouse and Christ Church, Oxford, Michael concentrated on athletics. As a middle-distance runner, he was a member of the Oxford and Cambridge athletics team which visited America and Canada in 1937; and he gained his blue in 1938. He took a law degree the next year.

At the outbreak of war in 1939, Melford joined up with the 5th Anti-Tank Regiment, Royal Artillery. His first posting was at St Andrews, where with three two-pounder anti-tank guns he defended against invasion the sacred soil of the Royal and Ancient Golf Club. 'It was a quelling thought,' he wrote later. 'All the heroes of those and other days, if they wanted the Old Course to survive, were now helpless to do anything about it except to rely on a perfectly ghastly player with a slice which ranked high among the horrors of war or peace.' Melford was, however, able to report a distinct improvement in his putting. Subsequently, his unit was with the First Army in Tunisia and Egypt. Next came the Italian campaign, and by the Armistice he was a major in the tangled situation in the Balkans.

Melford's journalistic career began in 1946, as athletics correspondent of the *Observer*; he also worked for *The Field*. His work for the *Daily Telegraph* mostly concerned cricket and rugby football, although he covered the Olympic Games in Melbourne in 1956 and in Rome in 1960. As cricket correspondent he reported tours to all the Test-playing countries, a record which even I (who never ventured into Pakistan) could not match. He was a member of MCC and a presentable cricketer who played for Hampstead and the Nondescripts.

In 1990 Melford published *After the Interval*, a reflective history of cricket in the post-war years. Extremely fond of golf, and despite his self-disparagement a perfectly reputable player, he wrote an admirable history of Denham Golf Club. Peter May, a fellow Carthusian, was an old friend, and Melford acted as amanuensis for May's autobiography, *A Game Enjoyed* (1985). He was also in demand as editor of such titles as *Pick of The Cricketer* and *The Daily Telegraph Cricket Yearbook*. In addition, he was associate editor of the first (1966) edition of the encyclopaedic *The World of Cricket*.

Michael Melford was married to Lorna (*née* Powell); they had two daughters.

RON ROBERTS

He showed cricket round the world

Roberts, Ronald Arthur

b: 1927

d: Woking, 17 August 1965. Aged 38.

Ronald Arthur Roberts was a regular cricket correspondent to the *Daily Telegraph*, and a freelance writer of worldwide standing. A West Country journalist by training, Ron Roberts made the first of his 14 overseas tours when, as second string to Reuter's correspondent, he went to Australia and New Zealand with the South African team of 1952–53. From then until his premature death twelve years later he saw and reported more cricket in a larger assortment of countries than any man. He also organised and managed more; for no sooner had he established himself as a cricket writer than he threw himself with great zeal and much competence into the arranging of tours all over the Commonwealth and beyond. In this incredible ambition he displayed tireless energy and administrative skill.

In 1959 he took the first of his Commonwealth teams to South Africa. The following year came the second to Rhodesia, South Africa and Kenya. In 1962 his spring tour embraced Kenya, Rhodesia, Pakistan, New Zealand, Hong Kong and Bombay. That autumn a side under his management went to Greece, Rhodesia, Tanganyika, Kenya and Malaya. In 1963 he covered Bombay, South Africa and Nairobi, in 1964 organised and managed Yorkshire in the United States, Canada and Bermuda.

He went abroad with the MCC Australian team of 1954–55, and covered the New Zealand end of that tour for the *Daily Telegraph*. Since that date he has travelled with every MCC team, contributing to the *Daily Telegraph* and latterly the *Sunday Telegraph* either on his own or in partnership with Michael Melford or myself.

Now that his journeys are over one can regard Roberts's activities, compressed in this short spell, with wonder and admiration. They derived from a deep love of cricket and an affection for cricketers of whatever colour or creed. As a critic he was always stringent in defence of the highest standards. Yet he had the knack of being unequivocal without giving offence. A player himself, he knew the game was not as easy as it sometimes looks to elderly eyes in the press-box.

His chief contribution to cricket was his conception of bringing together men from different countries in one team to travel everywhere, to encourage the game in many places, and in so doing to break down the barriers of race and colour. He had a simple, disarming naturalness that persuaded famous West Indians, for instance, to venture with him to Southern Africa, and to be glad that they had gone. One can indeed scarcely think of a personality in the cricket world whose death will be mourned by so many: by his fellow journalists, by administrators of county clubs and provincial and national bodies, by his readers, and not least by the players of the fifties and sixties. In a decade he had become an institution.

In his youth he was a member of the committee of Somerset, and he was the author of *Sixty Years of Somerset Cricket*.

10

MASTERS OF SPIN

'TICH' FREEMAN
Wickets galore

Freeman, Alfred Percy   Professional

b: Lewisham, London, 17 May 1888   *Teams:* Kent, MCC, England

Career batting:
592-716-194-4961-66-9.50; *ct* 238-*st* 1
Bowling: 69577-3776-18.42

Test batting: 12-16-5-154-50*-14.00; *ct* 4
Bowling: 1707-66-25.86

d: Bearsted, Kent, 28 January 1965. Aged 76.

As the summers pass and we continue to lament the eclipse of English spin bowling the career of 'Tich' Freeman between the wars grows even more fantastical and the contrast between his county and Test records more extraordinary. His aggregate of 3,776 wickets is bettered only by Wilfred Rhodes's 4,187, and whereas the latter's victims were spread over 1,107 matches Freeman bowled in a mere 592. Freeman was reckoned often to buy his wickets regardless of runs scored. Yet the cost of his wickets at 18.42 runs each does not greatly exceed the frugal Rhodes's figure of 16.71. Cold figures too often deny airy assertions of this kind.

Again, Freeman was generally rated comparatively harmless against men quick on their feet. Well, Bradman was as nimble as anyone. In 1930 against Kent he made 18 (lbw b. Freeman) and 206 not out. Tich took six for 146 at a rate of exactly 2 runs an over. There was a famous match at Hastings when Sussex, and Duleep in particular, sought revenge for a too-late watering at the Mote which made them helpless against Freeman. The result was the second largest aggregate in a county match, Duleep making 115 and 246. Duleep used his feet to perfection and runs were cheap indeed – but Freeman had nine wickets at 26 runs apiece. The truth is that he was a master of flight who pushed the ball through more quickly against the best players, distinctly higher against the fast-footed.

In his day the selectors, of course, had quite a wide field of choice among leg-spinners, Freeman being one of eight who in 1930 had either played for England or were about to. It was logical to pick R. W. V. Robins as an all-rounder for the first two Tests against Australia in 1930. Freeman, however, both in 1928 and 1929 in three home Tests each against the West Indies and South Africa respectively, had much the best record: 22 wickets in each year, almost twice as many as anyone else. To have preferred Dick Tyldesley in 1930 to Freeman at Headingley (where Bradman made 309 undefeated on the first day) looks in retrospect a very strange decision. It seems as though Percy Chapman, who had not needed Freeman in the Australian Tests the previous winter, was not keen to have his services now.

In county cricket Freeman, though now forty, was at the peak of his success. Having taken between 102 and 194 wickets in the preceding eight summers, in 1928, a great year for batsmen incidentally, he took the unprecedented number of 304 wickets. In all the next six years he had over 250, and in 1935, 212. When in 1936 Freeman's bag dropped to a mere 110 – and costing 25 runs each at that – the county committee decided that enough was enough. Doug Wright, having watched and learned for several years as understudy, at 21 was given the full responsibility. Among various records was the unprecedented taking of all ten wickets three times. Only Jim Laker has had more than Tich's 17 in a match.

Although short in height, Freeman was broad in the chest and a quick cover-point fielder with the peculiar habit of constantly hitching up his trousers. The fact that he lasted so well was probably because he was over 30 and his body fully developed before he became a regular in the Kent side. It is to the discredit of the selection committees concerned that his Test career consisted of only 12 matches (in which he had the perfectly respectable figures of 66 wickets at 25 runs each) and that it ended in 1929 when he had six highly fruitful years ahead. He played a little League cricket for Walsall before finally taking his boots off and naming his house Dunbowlin.

JIM LAKER

He made history laconically

Laker, James Charles   Professional

b: Frizinghall, Bradford, Yorkshire, 9 February 1922

Sch: Salts High School   *Teams:* Surrey, MCC, England,
                                    Commonwealth, Cavaliers, Essex

Career batting:
450-548-108-7304-113-16.60; hundreds 2-*ct* 270
Bowling: 35791-1944-18.41

Test batting:
46-63-15-676-63-14.08; *ct* 12
Bowling: 4101-193-21.24

d: Putney, London, 23 April 1986. Aged 64.

The name of Jim Laker, the taker of an unprecedented 19 wickets in a match and 46 in an England-Australia series, is secure for ever in the world of cricket. The word 'great' is sometimes over-used in the case of a cricketer. In his case it can be claimed without argument. On easy-paced pitches overseas some might prefer as off-spin bowlers either Lance Gibbs of Guyana and West Indies or Hugh Tayfield of Natal, Transvaal and South Africa. But when English pitches are brought into an assessment of merit there can be no argument.

Laker's bowling against the 1956 Australians in the Old Trafford Test is a memorial safe for all time:

1st innings	16.4–4–37–9
2nd innings	51.2–23–53–10

At the other end Tony Lock, the left-arm other half of the Surrey spin partnership, bowled one over more than Laker for a return of

219

one wicket for 106. No one had taken more than 17 wickets in any sort of first-class match, let alone a Test. But then no one had, or has since, taken all ten wickets twice in a season, and Laker's figures for Surrey's match against the Australians at The Oval in May had been: 46–18–88–10

On what sort of pitches were these incredible things done, the reader will ask. Well, at The Oval it was dry and the Australians made 259 and Surrey followed with 347. It had become somewhat dusty when the Australians in their second innings were bowled out for 107. It was then Lock's seven for 49 which enabled Surrey to win by ten wickets. Thus they became the first county to lower Australia's colours since 1912.

In the Old Trafford Test, England had the luck of the toss and on a dry surface made 459. In the latter part of their innings dust could occasionally be seen where the ball pitched. The *Daily Telegraph* correspondent described the surface on which Laker and Lock then performed as 'awkward and in spasms treacherous'. On the second afternoon Australia collapsed to 84 all out, and following on had at the close made 59 for two. Laker had all the help he needed, setting his opponents an examination against which they succumbed with a feverish mixture of timidity and desperation. Heavy rain had made the pitch sluggish and unresponsive on the fourth and last day, and Laker needed all his abundant skill to bring England to victory with an hour to spare. The scene is still clear enough 40-odd years on, and not least of the hero strolling back to the pavilion, sweater over his shoulder, rather as if he were coming back from the nets.

Laker was Yorkshire-born and Yorkshire cricketer in outlook, but he passed through their hands without engagement and in 1946 was playing for Catford in south London when Andrew Kempton, an influential Surrey man, arranged a trial for him at The Oval.

He was 25 but raw in experience when chosen to tour with Gubby Allen's MCC side to the West Indies in 1947–48. With 36 wickets for 27 runs each on perfect pitches against an intrinsically stronger team Laker made an auspicious start. As the only regular spinner in the England side in 1948 at Headingley, the fact that on a dusty pitch Australia scored 404 on the last day to win was, however, long held against him. He took his hundred wickets a year inexpensively from 1948 to 1958, during which Surrey won seven successive Championships. Yet it was 1956 before he played in a whole series for England and only in the following winter in South Africa that he did so abroad.

In these later years he was bothered by sore, calloused and arthritic fingers, and in 1958 he first declined and later accepted to tour Australia with Peter May's side. Never an easy man to handle, he was now at odds with his county and Test captain and when the crucial fourth Test came round with England two down in the series, Laker, after a net on the morning of the match, declared himself unfit to play. Heading the bowling averages for the tour, he was not chosen for England in 1959 and at the end of that season announced his retirement.

From this pinnacle Laker's reputation took an uneven course. Early in 1960 a book *Over to Me* was published under his name though ghosted by Christopher Ford, a young agency cricket-writer. Its cricitisms gave such offence in official quarters that MCC cancelled his honorary membership and Surrey withdrew his pavilion pass. From 1962 to 1964 he played 30 matches for Essex, taking 111 wickets and showing much of his old mastery when the conditions were right. There was irony in that he who had always resented the class system as applied to cricket, and the privilege accorded to amateurs and denied to the professionals, played in 1962 as an amateur. (That winter the distinction was abolished.)

Laker had quickly regretted *Over to Me*. He took to journalism and in 1969 was recruited by the BBC to give commentaries on TV. He at once showed a natural aptitude for it. In fact the last 16 years of his life must have been, thanks to his TV work, the happiest. Tony Lewis, who worked with him on TV for many years summed up his attributes for the benefit of Alan Hill's admirable biography:

> As a commentator, Jim read the game brilliantly. There was always the right emphasis. He never gave anything more than it was worth. He did not hold back from praise but he would explain exactly how that lay in the firmament.

I would subscribe completely to that testimonial, adding that when there was nothing to say, as it were, he didn't say it. Like Richie Benaud and in the golf world Henry Longhurst, he was a master of 'the golden pause'.

His privileges at Lord's and The Oval were duly restored, and he had become a highly respected figure long before his illness and death in 1986. As with other great Surrey cricketers, a Thanksgiving Service was held for him in Southwark Cathedral.

TONY LOCK

Man of three careers

Lock, Graham Anthony Richard   Professional

b: Limpsfield, Surrey, 5 July 1929

Sch: Limpsfield School   *Teams:* Surrey, Leicestershire, MCC, England, Western Australia

Career batting:
654-812-161-10342-89-15.88; *ct* 830
Bowling: 54709-2844-19.23

Test batting:
49-63-9-742-89-13.74; *ct* 59
Bowling: 4451-174-25.58

d: Perth, Western Australia, 23 March 1995. Aged 65.

Tony Lock will be chiefly remembered as the left-arm counterpart to the right-arm off-spinner, Jim Laker, in the all-conquering Surrey sides of the 1950s. That, however, is only an instalment in the story. Having played 385 matches in 17 years with the county of his birth, he moved in 1965 to Leicestershire where he showed himself a fervent and formidable captain, taking them in 1967 to second place in the Championship, a lofty height to which they had never previously aspired.

Yet there was a third phase no less remarkable than the others. Disappointed at not having been chosen for the MCC side to Australia in 1962–63, he went there on his own account and then enjoyed 9 seasons at Perth during which he led Western Australia to their first ever Sheffield Shield title. He played in the subtropical heat until he was 41.

Lock brought to his cricket a determination and burning enthusiasm to which both Leicestershire and Western Australia heartily responded. He was, too, a brilliant close fielder: hence his tally of 830 catches, mostly at short-leg. Lock's Test career contained five MCC tours and 49 Tests at home spread over 16 seasons.

His career would have been much smoother but for the years in which his action was more than suspect. He was unlucky in that after a beginning on orthodox slow left-arm spinning lines he spent a winter at an indoor school with a low top net. Hence his reliance on a faster trajectory with an accompanying sharper spin. He was no-balled a few times for throwing both at home and in the West Indies, and both selectors and we critics must share blame for failing to air the problem.

In fact it was Lock himself who in New Zealand at the conclusion of the MCC Australasian tour of 1958–59 saw a film of himself in action and was horrified at the sight. There was a successful purge on suspect actions following the ICC meeting of 1960, wherein the leading spirits were Gubby Allen in this country and Don Bradman in Australia. No special scrutiny was, however, directed at Lock for he had reverted to the slower style of his young days which was beyond reproach.

It needed determination and hard work to make the further transition effective, but Lock was not short of either virtue. He transformed his action, and though less effective than before in England he took a record number of 316 wickets in his nine Australian summers. Following an accident to Fred Titmus in the West Indies in 1967–68, he was summoned to the colours for the last time by the captain, Colin Cowdrey, whereupon he made his highest Test score of 89 and played a full part in the last English series victory in the West Indies.

He took 100 wickets in a season 14 times, and all ten for 54 against Kent at Blackheath, 16 in the match. In 1957 his bag was 212. He took four hat-tricks. Yet of all his feats nothing was more extraordinary than that at Old Trafford in helpful conditions he took only one wicket while Laker was gathering 19.

IAN PEEBLES

Artist with ball and pen

Peebles, Ian Alexander Ross   Amateur

b: Aberdeen, Scotland, 20 January 1908

Sch: Glasgow Academy   *Teams:* Middlesex, Oxford U., Scotland,
                                  MCC, England, Cahn to Ceylon,
                                  Tennyson to India

Career batting:
251-330-101-2213-58-9.66; *ct* 172
Bowling: 19738-923-21.38

Test batting:
13-17-8-98-26-10.88; *ct* 5
Bowling: 1391-45-30.91

d: Speen, Buckinghamshire, 27 February 1980. Aged 72.

To say that Ian Peebles was a cricketer to his fingertips is doubly true in that he ranked high both as a spinner of the ball and, from the moment of his retirement to the end of his days, as a writer on the game.

It was the sight of the 1921 Australians as a boy of 13 in Glasgow that fired Peebles's ambition to be a cricketer. When, aged 19, he went on holiday to London and presented himself at Aubrey Faulkner's School of Cricket, that great all-rounder and coach, seeing the possibilities, offered him a secretarial job there. Plum Warner was equally enthusiastic: hence came a place for this untried youth with sharp leg-spin, top-spin and googly engendered by a high, flowing action, in the strong, but not representative, MCC side to South Africa of 1927–28.

On those matting pitches he took 34 wickets, and in 1929 he was one of the three Middlesex amateurs with N. Haig and R. W. V. Robins, who took 100 wickets. Going up to Oxford that autumn, Peebles in 1930 reached his peak. He took thirteen for 237 against

Cambridge and seven for 120 for the Gentlemen at Lord's. He was accordingly chosen to play for England in the fourth Test against Australia at Old Trafford.

There he briefly halted Don Bradman's triumphal progress on a slow but not spiteful turner. Missed off him at first slip, Bradman was soon caught at second slip for 14, and though in the decisive Oval Test Bradman, with an innings of 232, brought his tally for the series to 974, Peebles had the remarkable analysis of 71-8-204-6. Peebles played seven more times for England in the next 12 months, but torn fibres in his right shoulder now hindered his leg-spin, and thenceforward he was always an accurate bowler but seldom a destroyer. After sporadic appearances for Middlesex, he had a season as captain in 1939, and after the war bowled gallantly on in club cricket despite the loss of his left (and leading) eye in a bombing raid.

As cricket correspondent of the *Sunday Times* Ian won a wide following as a reporter and, especially, as an essayist of a style and humour distinctly his own. He contributed also to the *Observer*, the *Guardian*, and *The Cricketer*, and wrote several books, of which the best, his autobiography, *Spinner's Yarn*, won the Cricket Society's Literary Award. He belonged to that happy breed of sportsmen with a multitude of friends and never an enemy.

HUGH TAYFIELD

Just like a metronome

Tayfield, Hugh Joseph   Amateur

b: Durban, South Africa, 30 January 1929

Sch: Durban High School   *Teams:* Natal, Rhodesia, Transvaal,
                                        South Africa

Career batting:
187-259-47-3668-77-17.30; *ct* 149
Bowling: 18890-864-21.86

Test batting:
37-60-9-862-75-16.90; *ct* 26
Bowling: 4405-170-25.91

d: Durban, South Africa, 25 February 1994. Aged 65.

Hugh Tayfield took 170 wickets in Test matches, more than any other South African. As an off-spinner he rates high among the best of the moderns, Lance Gibbs, Jim Laker, Fred Titmus and E. A. S. Prasanna. None of these in their separate ways, I think, exercised in four successive series in the mid-fifties such a consistent dominance as did Tayfield. His South African generation inherited an endemic lack of self-belief that was in particularly strong contrast with Australian attitudes.

At Durban in 1950 Tayfield on a difficult pitch took seven for 23, the best figures of his life, Australia being bowled out for 75. Despite a lead of 236, South Africa were too timid to enforce the follow-on and lost the match humiliatingly. Two years later Louis Duffus, the leading South African critic, campaigned in favour of cancelling their impending tour of Australia. But a forceful leader emerged in J. E. Cheetham who, with a combative Tayfield shouldering the main attacking burden, astonished the cricket world by halving the series.

Tayfield's method involved two straight short legs stationed together at 15 yards' range in a six-three field with inviting off-side gaps. From a high action and delivering from directly over the stumps, he aimed at middle-and-leg with accuracy and subtle variations of spin and flight. He took 30 wickets on that Australian tour, 21 at home against New Zealand in 1953–54, 26 in England in 1955 and finally 37 when England toured the Union in 1956–57. That this was almost the slowest-scoring series on record (conducted at less than 30 runs per hour) was chiefly due, so far as England were concerned, to the stranglehold imposed by Tayfield and Trevor Goddard.

Tayfield's influence grew even more pronounced as the Tests progressed. At Durban, where his match analysis was 61.7-31-90-9, he bowled 137 successive balls without a run scored, then a world first-class record. One was fervently willing the batsmen to come down the pitch, yet recognising that his control made it a hazardous exercise. In the fourth Test at Johannesburg when England, with eight wickets in hand, only needed a further 85 runs to win the match and rubber, they failed by 18. Tayfield bowled 35 consecutive eight-ball overs, taking nine for 113. A return of six for 78 in the last Test enabled South Africa to square the series and Tayfield, with 37 wickets, to establish a South African record. His 4.6 wickets per Test is the highest striking rate among post-war spinners, superior to Laker, Ramadhin and Warne. At his best he was a great bowler.

J. C. WHITE

Success in Australia

White, John Cornish   Amateur

b: Holford, Somerset, 19 February 1891

Sch: Taunton   *Teams:* Somerset, MCC, England

Career batting:
472-765-102-12202-192-18.40; hundreds 6-*ct* 426
Bowling: 43759-2356-18.57

Test batting:
15-22-9-239-29-18.38; *ct* 6
Bowling: 1581-49-32.26

d: Yarde Farm, Combe-Florey, Somerset, 2 May 1961. Aged 70.

J. C. White was an estimable cricketer and a modest, most likeable man. His career for Somerset spanned 28 years and he was captain between 1927–31, succeeding the redoubtable John Daniell. He was president of Somerset CCC at the time of his death. Jack White was a subtle, slow left-arm bowler more notable for command of length and flight than for his powers of spin. It was this quality, added to his capacity to bowl economically for long periods, that caused his selection to go with MCC to Australia in 1928–29 in his 38th year. Sir Jack Hobbs (who was co-opted to the selection committee for that tour) is credited with having advocated his choice, which came as a considerable surprise.

In the Tests he pinned down the best Australian batsmen in a remarkable way. With 25 wickets for 30 runs apiece he complemented the efforts of Larwood, Tate and Geary and helped England to a spectacular triumph. In the Adelaide Test came the great trial of his stamina when in much heat he bowled 124 overs. Australians still speak of the astonishing accuracy that enabled him, despite the relatively short square boundaries at the Adelaide Oval, to bowl with only two men on the leg-side. His batting was stubborn rather than graceful but it was effective enough twice to bring him the double of a thousand runs and a hundred wickets. He took 100 wickets 14 times and, overall, no fewer than 2,356.

In 1919 he took 16 wickets in a day at Bath against Worcestershire. They seem to have been his rabbits, for two years later he took all 10 wickets against them at Worcester. These were shining feats but it was his day-to-day consistency which made him such a stand-by for a county of small resources. He played for England at home against Australia, South Africa and the West Indies, and went to South Africa with MCC in 1930–31. But the Australian tour was his finest hour.

DOUG WRIGHT

Seven hat-tricks

Wright, Douglas Vivian Parson   Professional

b: Sidcup, Kent, 21 August 1914

Sch: St Nicholas Parish School, Chislehurst.   *Teams:* Kent, MCC,
England

Career batting:
497-703-225-5903-84*-12.34; *ct* 182
Bowling: 49307-2056-23.98

Test batting:
34-39-13-289-45-11.11; *ct* 10
Bowling: 4224-108-39.11

d: Canterbury, 13 November 1998. Aged 84.

D.V. P. Wright of Kent and England was on his best days a uniquely dangerous bowler of quick leg-breaks and googlies and on his not so good days a generous contributor to the general entertainment. His third, unusual Christian name, Parson, might be seen as a reminder of a smiling benevolence towards all and sundry which was truly evangelistic. Doug was surrounded in the Kent XIs of his time by similarly delightful characters – Bryan Valentine, Les Ames, Gerry Chalk and Godfrey Evans not least – men who ensured that, however keen, the game was always played in the right spirit. Doug's action was singular and unforgettable, described thus by Ray Robinson: 'Wright's 10 strides are of assorted sizes, a few short steps, five long bounds and a quick finish ending in a leap. Just before that he spreads his arms wide then lifts both overhead as a preliminary to his full circle delivery.' Note the full circle, as essential to truly sharp spin as strong fingers, developed in his case by long hours of bowling in the Indoor School (the first of all) at Hammersmith run by the great South

African all-rounder, wrist-spin bowler and coach, Aubrey Faulkner.

Doug and I met first at the School, as he used to remind me because I apparently middled a straight drive which, but for a jump in the nick of time, might have jeopardised his budding manhood. This fluky incident aside, he always said how much he owed – as did many other excellent cricketers – to Faulkner's tuition. He was equally lucky, of course, in being brought gradually into the Kent team alongside the most prolific of all wrist-spinners, Tich Freeman, and another master of the art in C. S. (Father) Marriott.

When after Freeman's retirement (having taken 'only' 107 wickets for Kent in 1936) Wright, at the age of 22, took over the wrist-spin, he responded with 107 wickets in 1937 and in 1938 won the first of his 34 Test caps for England. He remained the mainspring of the Kent attack until by 1956 his energies – which in his last three years included the captaincy of a struggling side – finally gave out. When it really mattered he was well above the rabbit class with the bat, and was a competent fielder with a very safe pair of hands. Ten times he took 100 wickets, and in 1947 he took 177. At Bristol against Gloucestershire he once had 9 for 47, and against Somerset at Bath 16 in the match for 80. How 'unplayable' he could sometimes be is attested by his world record of seven hat-tricks. Godfrey Evans's sparkling wicket-keeping to him added to the crowds' attractions, while when he was away Derek Ufton made a thoroughly efficient deputy.

I must now address the curiosity that his record in Test cricket was such a poor reflection of his value to England. In two visits each to Australia and South Africa plus his Tests at home he took 108 wickets at 39 runs each. Yet until Alec Bedser's first years of greatness his opponents feared Wright much more than any other bowler.

At Headingley in 1938, when Hammond belatedly put him on in the second innings, he took the wickets of Bradman, McCabe and Hassett in five overs. *Wisden* thought that his appearance earlier might well have won the match for England who, with their overwhelming win at The Oval following, would have recaptured the Ashes. Hammond, never a good or sympathetic leader, was Wright's captain in his first three major Test series. At Sydney in 1946–47, Yardley having taken over the captaincy, Wright took 7 for 105 in the first innings and in the second had Bradman palpably missed at slip when 2, after which he steered Australia to a hard-won victory by five wickets. But for the dropped catch the series would very likely have ended 2–1, not 3–0. When England at last in 1951 at Melbourne won their first post-war victory over Australia, his bowling of Hassett with the perfect leg-break turned the match.

In the Second World War he served as Lieutenant in the Royal Artillery. Too self-deprecatory to be a strong captain, his temperament and inexhaustible good nature made him an ideal coach. He was highly regarded at Charterhouse, where he served in succession to George Geary from 1959 to 1971. His final coaching was at the University of Kent and in the indoor school at Canterbury, his spiritual home.

INDEX